WINNING
TRACK
AND FIELD
FOR GIRLS

WINNING
TRACK
AND FIELD
FOR GIRLS

ED HOUSEWRIGHT

Foreword by
BUZZ ANDREWS
Former nationally ranked decathlete and Olympic coach

Photography by
KEVIN MARTIN

A MOUNTAIN LION BOOK

☑®
Facts On File, Inc.

To my daughter, Elyse,
who taught me to enjoy girls' sports.

WINNING TRACK AND FIELD FOR GIRLS

Copyright © 2004 by Mountain Lion, Inc.

Facts On File, Inc.
132 West 31st Street
New York NY 10001

Library of Congress Cataloging-in-Publication Data

Housewright, Ed, 1941–
    Winning track and field for girls / Ed Housewright; foreword by
    Buzz Andrews.
        p. cm.
    Includes bibliographical references and index.
    ISBN 0-8160-5231-X (hard : alk. paper)
    1. Track and field for women. I. Title.
    GV1060.8.H68 2004
    796.42′082—dc21   2003049241

Facts On File books are available at special discounts when purchased in bulk quantities for businesses, associations, institutions, or sales promotions. Please call our Special Sales Department in New York at (212) 967-8800 or (800) 322-8755.

You can find Facts On File on the World Wide Web at
http://www.factsonfile.com

Text design by Erika K. Arroyo
Cover design by Nora Wertz

Printed in the United States of America

VB FOF 10 9 8 7 6 5 4 3 2

This book is printed on acid-free paper.

CONTENTS

Foreword   xiii
Acknowledgments   xv
Introduction   xvi

1 HISTORY   **1**

2 SPRINTS   **5**

The Basics   6
Technique   7
  The Start   7
  Acceleration   11
  Full Stride   12
  Finish   12
Records   13
  100 Meters   13
  200 Meters   13
  400 Meters   14
Faults and Fixes   14
Drills   15
  To Improve Starts   15
  To Improve Muscle Tone and Flexibility   15
  To Improve Acceleration and
    Build Endurance   17
  To Improve Stride Length and
    Consistency   17
  Games to Liven Up Training   18
Superstar: Florence Griffith-Joyner   19
Sample Workouts   20
  100, 200 Meters (Off-Season)   20
  100, 200 Meters (Early Season)   21

100, 200 Meters (Mid-Season) 22
400 Meters (Off-Season) 22
400 Meters (Early Season) 23
400 Meters (Mid-Season) 24
Injuries 24
Superstar: Marion Jones 26

3 HURDLES   **28**

The Basics 29
Technique 30
Records 33
100-Meter Hurdles 33
400-Meter Hurdles 33
Faults and Fixes 34
Drills 35
High-Stepping 35
Jogging 35
Wall Exercise 35
Leading Leg Drill 37
Trailing Leg Drill 37
Chalk Drill 37
Add-Ons 38
Uphill Runs 38
Stair Hop 38
Sample Workouts 39
100-Meter Hurdles (Off-Season) 39
100-Meter Hurdles (Early Season) 39
Superstar: Gail Devers 40
100-Meter Hurdles (Mid-Season) 41
400-Meter Hurdles (Off-Season) 42
400-Meter Hurdles (Early Season) 42
400-Meter Hurdles (Mid-Season) 43
Superstar: Kim Batten 44

4 MIDDLE-DISTANCE AND LONG-DISTANCE RACES   **45**

The Basics 46
Technique 47
Records 48
800 Meters 48
1,500 Meters 49
3,000 Meters 49

Faults and Fixes 49
Drills 51
    Pace Practice 51
    Time Travel 51
    Interval Sprints 51
    Pyramid Sprints 51
    Cross-Country Training 51
    Uphill Runs 51
    Hurdle Hops 51
    Underwater Running 52
Sample Workouts 52
    800, 1,500, 3,000 Meters (Off-Season) 52
    800, 1,500, 3,000 Meters (Early Season) 53
    800, 1,500, 3,000 Meters (Mid-Season) 54
Superstars: Mary Decker and Zola Budd 55

5 RELAYS   57

The Basics 58
Technique 59
    Upsweep 59
    Downsweep 61
    4 × 400 Meters 62
Responsibilities of Each Runner in the
    4 × 100 Relay 63
    Lead Runner 63
    Second Runner 63
    Third Runner 63
    Fourth Runner 63
Responsibilities of Each Runner in the
    4 × 400 Relay 64
    Lead Runner 64
    Second Runner 64
    Third Runner 64
    Fourth Runner 64
Records 64
    4 × 100 Meter Relay 65
    4 × 400 Meter Relay 65
    4 × 800 Meter Relay 65
Faults and Fixes 66
Drills 67
    Bottle Drill 67

Bounce Drill   67
Standing Handoffs   67
Jogging Handoffs   68
Acceleration Drill   69
Hit the Spot   69
Superstars: The Record-Setting American
  4 × 100 Relay Team   69
Sample Workouts   70
  4 × 100 Meter Relay (Off-Season)   70
  4 × 100 Meter Relay (Early Season)   71
  4 × 100 Meter Relay (Mid-Season)   72
  4 × 400 Meter Relay (Off-Season)   73
  4 × 400 Meter Relay (Early Season)   73
  4 × 400 Meter Relay (Mid-Season)   74

6 JUMPING EVENTS   76

High Jump   77
  The Basics   78
  Technique   78
    Approach   78
    Takeoff   81
    Clearing the Bar   82
  Records   83
  Faults and Fixes   83
  Drills   84
    One-Legged Hurdle Hops   84
    Single-Leg Dips   84
    Beginning Jumping   85
    Figure Eights   85
    High-Stepping   85
    Bounding   85
    Approach Practice   86
  Sample Workouts   86
    High Jump (Off-Season)   86
    High Jump (Early Season)   87
    High Jump (Mid-Season)   88
Long Jump   88
  The Basics   89
  Technique   90
    Approach   90

    Takeoff 91

    Airborne Action 91

  Records 93

  Faults and Fixes 93

  Drills 94

    Run-Ups 94

    Lunges 94

    Single-Leg Hops 95

    Standing Long Jump 95

    Jumping Rope 95

    Step-Ups 95

  Sample Workouts 97

    Long Jump (Off-Season) 97

    Long Jump (Early Season) 97

    Long Jump (Mid-Season) 98

Triple Jump 99

  The Basics 99

  Technique 100

    Hop 100

    Step 101

    Jump 102

  Records 104

  Faults and Fixes 104

  Drills 105

    Bounding 105

    Box Stepping 105

    Box Jumping 106

    Hurdle Hops 106

  Sample Workouts 107

    Triple Jump (Off-Season) 107

    Triple Jump (Early Season) 107

    Triple Jump (Mid-Season) 108

Pole Vault 109

  The Basics 109

  Technique 110

    Grip and Pole Carry 111

    Approach 112

    Pole Plant and Takeoff 112

    Clearing the Bar 114

  Records 115

  Faults and Fixes 115

Drills | 116
    Rope Climb | 116
    Rope Swing | 116
    Backward Handstand | 116
    Swing and Rotate | 116
    Back Pushes | 117
Sample Workouts | 117
    Pole Vault (Off-Season) | 117
    Pole Vault (Early Season) | 118
    Pole Vault (Mid-Season) | 118
Superstar: Stacy Dragila | 119

7   THROWING EVENTS | **120**

Shot Put | 121
    The Basics | 121
    Technique | 122
        Glide | 122
        Spin | 122
    Records | 125
    Faults and Fixes | 125
Success Story: Michelle Carter | 126
    Drills | 127
        Simple Lift | 127
        Wrist Flips | 127
        Basketball Throws Against a Wall | 127
        Basketball Throws for Distance | 128
        Shot Put from Standing Position | 128
        Gliding Practice | 129
    Sample Workouts | 129
        Shot Put (Off-Season) | 129
        Shot Put (Early Season and Mid-Season) | 129
Discus | 130
    The Basics | 130
    Technique | 131
        Grip | 131
        Set-Up and Throw | 131
    Records | 134
    Faults and Fixes | 134
    Drills | 135
        Arm Swing | 135
        Sitting Throw | 135

Step and Sling 135
Complete Throw with Rubber Ring 135
Spin Practice 135
Sample Workouts 136
Discus (Off-Season, Early Season,
and Mid-Season) 136
Discus (Early Season and
Mid-Season) 136
Javelin 137
The Basics 137
Technique 137
Grip 137
Approach and Throw 138
Records 141
Faults and Fixes 141
Drills 142
Basketball Throw 142
Step and Throw 142
Four-Step Throw 142
Standing Throw with a Javelin 143
Five-Step Throw with Javelin 144
Sample Workouts 144
Javelin (Off-Season) 144
Javelin (Early Season and
Mid-Season) 145

8 HEPTATHLON, CROSS-COUNTRY, MARATHON, AND TRIATHLON 146

Heptathlon 147
The Basics 148
Success Story: Diana and Julie Pickler 149
Cross-Country 150
Marathon 153
Superstar: Joan Benoit Samuelson 155
Triathlon 157

9 MENTAL PREPARATION AND NUTRITION 160

Mental Preparation 160
Nutrition 162

10 STRETCHES AND WEIGHT LIFTING   **165**

    Stretching   165
        Types of Stretches   165
            Hurdler's Stretch   165
            Palms on Ground   166
            Leg Extensions   166
            Ankle Pull   167
            Groin Stretch   167
            Torso Bend   167
            Leg Crossover   167
            Body Lean   167
            Torso Twist   169
            Back Roll   170
            Neck Roll   170
    Weight Lifting   170
        Lower Body   171
            Leg Extension   171
            Leg Curl   171
            Leg Press   172
            Squat   172
            Calf Raise   172
        Upper Body   172
            Bench Press   172
            Shoulder Press   172
            Upright Rowing   172
            Lat Pull-Downs   173
            Dips   173
            Biceps Curls   173
            Triceps Pull-Downs   173
            Crunches   173

Associations and Websites   174
Further Reading   175
Index   177

FOREWORD

Track and field has been part of my life for almost 40 years. It's taught me—and the athletes I've coached—countless life lessons.

Through track, I've learned to set goals, work hard to achieve them and persevere when I faced setbacks. The same can be said of the hundreds of young men and women I've had the pleasure to coach in Texas and Arkansas.

My love of track kept me from veering into trouble. I knew that if I stayed out all night partying and abusing my body, I could never do well in track. Success in track meant more to me than a few hours of reckless fun with the guys.

The dedication I learned in track carried over into academics. I grew up in the tiny town of Hope, Arkansas, but graduated with a bachelor's degree in marketing and management from Ouachita Baptist University in Arkadelphia, Arkansas, where I was on a full track scholarship. (I competed in the decathlon against Bruce Jenner, the 1976 Olympic gold medal winner.) I followed up my bachelor's degree with a master's in physical education two years later.

Early on, I knew that I wanted to devote my life to coaching track, and I'm glad I did. I've coached other sports from time to time, but I think track can teach you the most. For one thing, it's primarily an individual sport. You control whether you win or lose. You can't blame a teammate for missing an assignment or an official for blowing a call.

Success in track and field can be measured—just like success in life. The stopwatch and tape measure don't lie. Sports that are judged subjectively, such as gymnastics or figure skating, have never appealed to me. So a judge gives you a 6.0? What does that really mean?

When I competed, I tried to improve my performance every time I stepped on the track. I didn't need a coach or judge to tell me if I had done so—I could look at the stopwatch.

Track isn't an easy sport. I require my athletes to train for hours and hours, although I know they would often rather be somewhere else. But I encourage them to remember why they're pushing their bodies so hard. For some, their goal may be a winning district championship, setting a school record, or earning a college scholarship.

Others may not have the talent to realistically hold those aspirations. But they can still set goals—their *own* goals. For instance, they can work to lower their time, increase their height, or improve their distance at every meet. They can commit to staying on the track team, even if they aren't a star.

I've had many students tell me years after they graduate that the biggest lesson they learned from track was perseverance. Some, for example, have told me they enrolled in college and did poorly at first. They wanted to quit but then remembered the satisfaction they had gained from sticking with track. That memory inspired them to stay in college and pursue their career dream.

I've received cards, e-mails, and telephone calls from former students around the world who now have rewarding jobs. No one has ever told me that they regretted competing in track and field.

For many young people who participate in track, fitness becomes a lifelong pursuit. If you learn to appreciate a conditioned body at a young age, you're not likely to abuse your body and let it deteriorate as you age.

Track competition doesn't have to end in high school. Today, there are numerous "masters" meets in which people of all ages can go up against others their age. I recently coached a 67-year-old woman who set the world record in her age group in the pole vault. She cleared seven feet! She was as proud as any 17-year-old I've ever coached.

To me, that says a lot about track and field. Whatever your age, whatever your ability, you can find an event to call your own. You'll enjoy the benefits now and for years to come.

Good luck!

—Buzz Andrews
Former nationally ranked decathlete
and Olympic coach

ACKNOWLEDGMENTS

We could not have done this book without the help of others. We would like to thank the following young women whom we photographed to demonstrate track and field techniques: Stephanie Best, Angeline Guido, Caresir Hamilton, Jessica Moore, Dawnyel Newhouse, Shawntel Newhouse, Rachel Rene Redding, and Ashley Scott.

INTRODUCTION

It's easy to understand the popularity of track and field. The sport includes a wide range of activities: running, jumping, and throwing events—one of which (or more) will appeal to almost anyone who is athletically inclined.

People who are blessed with speed are drawn to the sprinting events, such as the 100- and 200-meter races. Youths who lack blazing speed but have more endurance can do well in middle-distance events, such as the 800- and 1,500-meter runs. Others choose long-distance races, such as 3,000 meters, that test the limits of stamina and determination.

Each event offers a unique challenge and unique training methods.

Track may seem like a simple sport—just run as fast as you can to the finish line. That impression is incorrect. Flat-out speed is obviously a plus. But athletes competing in running events of all lengths must learn proper technique—and in some cases strategy—to perform their best.

The same is true for the jumping events (high jump, long jump, triple jump, and pole vault) and throwing events (shot put, discus, and javelin). Proper form and good coaching in these events can also propel an athlete with moderate natural talent—and a will to win—past an athlete with an abundance of innate ability.

That's where *Winning Track and Field for Girls* comes in.

Consider it an instruction manual for young athletes and coaches alike. The book thoroughly explains each event and describes the type of athlete that normally excels in it. Every athlete has strengths and weaknesses, and every event has special demands. *Winning Track and Field for Girls* offers customized training programs for each event, including drills and sample workouts, that give every girl a chance for success.

This isn't a book you read one time and put away. It's intended to be referred to time and time again, like any reference book. Find the event you're interested in, study the instructional text and photos, and then try to copy what you've read. Naturally, you won't do it perfectly the first time. That's why you should consult the book again.

It's best to review the material right after a workout, when your performance and mistakes are fresh in your mind. By doing so, you'll remember tips to try next time. It's a good sign if you refer back to *Winning Track and Field for Girls* over and over. It shows that you're serious about improving and not content to make mistakes.

Winning Track and Field for Girls is intended to be a concise overview of the sport. It's not an exhaustive treatment of every facet of track and field. Once you've read the book, you can consult more specialized books and articles to supplement your knowledge. You should also talk to coaches and fellow athletes to benefit from their experience. Your coach will be impressed if you understand the basics of track and field when you show up for your first practice.

Each chapter of the book covers two or more similar events. Photos and illustrations demonstrate key points, such as correct foot position, body lean, arm action and hand placement. Some readers may be surprised at the space devoted to mechanics, but resist the temptation to skim over this material.

Normally, athletes who master the fundamentals are the ones who win. Over time, proper technique becomes second nature—muscle memory takes over. That's the goal of training. In the heat of competition, a hurdler, for instance, doesn't want to count her steps and think about leg extension as she clears a hurdle. She mastered those details during her practice.

At a meet, it's show time. That's when the hours of practice and preparation—and correction from a coach—pay off. At the same time, track and field should always be fun—even practice. *Winning Track and Field for Girls* offers drills that can liven up training and simulate meets while strengthening fundamentals.

Here, then, is an overview of the book.

Chapter 1 discusses the history of track and field, dating back to ancient Greece. In the first Olympics, women were barred from competition. Over the centuries, women have overcome stereotypes and bias to gain equal footing with men. Today, women compete in virtually all the same events as men.

Chapter 2 focuses on sprints, the 100-, 200-, and 400-meter races. The similarities and differences of each race are discussed.

Chapter 3 takes up the 100- and 200-meter hurdles. These events require the speed of a sprinter and coordination of a high jumper.

Chapter 4 moves to middle-distance races (800 and 1,500 meters) and the long-distance race (3,000 meters).

Chapter 5 covers relay races, the 4 × 100 and 4 × 400. Relays are among the most challenging events in track and field. Proper technique and tireless practice are necessary to exchange the baton smoothly in a pressure-filled meet. A dropped baton usually ends any hope of winning.

Chapter 6 outlines the jumping events high jump, long jump, triple jump, and pole vault. They may have a common denominator, but they involve dramatically different mechanics.

Chapter 7 discusses the shot put, discus, and javelin—the throwing events. Some people assume that a girl must be large and imposing to excel in these events. Not true. A smaller girl with sound fundamentals and good coaching can often out-throw a bigger competitor. Again, proper form and dedication are the keys.

Chapter 8 deals with the heptathlon, a taxing two-day competition that consists of a total of seven running, jumping, and throwing events. It's the equivalent of the decathlon for boys. The heptathlon gained prominence with the accomplishments of Jackie Joyner-Kersee. She won the silver medal in the 1984 Olympics and the gold in the 1988 and 1992 Games. This chapter also discusses cross-country, an event held in the fall during off-season for traditional track and field. It also touches on the marathon and triathlon, two high-endurance events.

Chapter 9, the last chapter, looks at mental preparation and nutrition. In recent years, elite athletes in all sports have utilized mental techniques, such as visualization, to maximize performance. Seeing yourself excel and imagining the conditions you will face can contribute greatly to success. Likewise, learning to handle disappointment can prevent a minor setback from derailing a young athlete's dreams.

Nutrition, like mental preparation, can be a building block for success. The phrase "you are what you eat" is largely true. Top athletes need a good fuel supply. Eating right, however, doesn't have to be complicated or require costly supplements with unknown side effects.

Sprinkled throughout each chapter are short profiles of prominent track athletes, such as Marion Jones, whose beaming smile became familiar to millions of viewers during the 2000 Olympics. She won the gold medal in the 100 meters, 200 meters, and 4 × 400 meter relay, and bronze in the long jump and 4 × 100 relay. She is the only female track athlete ever to win five medals in a single Olympics.

Winning Track and Field for Girls also includes memorable quotations from track athletes that can instruct and inspire. For instance, Florence Griffith-Joyner, who won three gold medals in the 1988 Olympics, once commented on her will to win, "When anyone tells me I can't do anything," she said, "I'm just not listening anymore."

Finally, each chapter lists event records, both world records and high school records by age group. These times and distances may seem intimidating, but they aren't intended to discourage or set unrealistic standards for beginners. Rather, they provide a benchmark for competition. Girls can enjoy track and field without ever approaching these marks.

One of the appeals of track is that it's both an individual and a team sport. An athlete may win her race and be justifiably proud. However, she can be just as proud to be part of a winning relay team in which members worked together to achieve a common goal.

Keep in mind that schools win track meets by compiling the most overall points based on individual events. Even athletes who fall short of their own expectations can share in the joy of a meet championship.

1
HISTORY

No sport has a longer, more illustrious history than track and field. Although rudimentary running and throwing competitions probably existed for centuries before, the first recorded track and field competitions were the Olympic Games that took place in Greece in 776 B.C.

The early Olympics were part of a major religious festival honoring Zeus, the chief Greek god. They had far fewer events than we do today, and only men were allowed to compete. Women were not even permitted to attend. If they did, they could be killed, according to some accounts.

After Greece fell to the Roman Empire ca. 140 B.C., the Olympics lost their religious significance and declined in stature. In A.D. 394, the Roman emperor Theodosius banned the Olympics, and no games were held for more than 1,500 years.

Track and field, however, survived. The sport was introduced in England in the 1100s and became widely popular in the 1800s. In 1864, Cambridge and Oxford Universities competed in the first intercollegiate track and field meet. A short time later, track came to the United States, and the first national championship was held here in 1876.

Twenty years later, the Olympics were reborn. The first modern Games were held, fittingly, in Athens, Greece, in 1896. They included more than 300 athletes from 13 countries, with track and field as the dominant sport. Just as in ancient times, women were not allowed to compete. The man who rekindled the Olympics, Baron Pierre de Coubertin of France, said they were intended to be "a solemn and periodic exaltation of male athleticism with . . . female applause as reward."

Women, however, refused to remain excluded. After the International Olympic Committee voted to uphold a ban on women's track and field in 1921, Alice Milliat, a Frenchwoman, organized the Women's Olympics in 1922. Athletes from five countries competed in front of 20,000 spectators in Paris.

The second Women's Olympics was held in Gothenburg, Sweden, in 1926, and 10 nations sent athletes. Finally, the International Olympic Committee relented and permitted five women's track and field events in the 1928 Olympics.

A breakthrough for women occurred with the accomplishments of Babe Didrikson in the 1932 Olympics in Los Angeles. She won the gold medal in the 80-meter sprint and javelin and took the silver in high jump. Didrikson was an outstanding all-around athlete who previously had excelled in basketball and swimming and later dominated the women's professional golf tour.

In addition, she was fiercely determined and spoke her mind in an age when women athletes were not widely accepted. She once said her goal was "to be the greatest athlete who ever lived." Before the 1932 Olympics, she boldly stated, "I came out here to beat everybody in sight, and that's what I'm going to do."

People were amazed at Babe's diverse talents. She seemed unbeatable at any sport she tried, including tennis, handball, bowling, and billiards. A reporter once asked if there was anything she didn't play. She replied, "Yeah, dolls."

Babe was the first female track athlete to capture widespread respect and admiration.

"She is beyond belief until you see her perform," legendary sports columnist Grantland Rice wrote. He added, she is "the most flawless section of muscle harmony, of complete mental and physical coordination, the world of sport has ever seen."

Progress for women's track and field remained slow, but steady. Gradually, more women began to compete, and barriers fell. In the 1952 Olympics, more than 500 women competed for the first time. Events that had been off limits to women became open.

During the 1956 Olympics, Wilma Rudolph became a household name. At only 16, she won a bronze medal in the 4 × 100 meter relay. Her achievement was even more remarkable considering that she had polio as a child and wore braces on her legs until she was nine. Once she began running, no one could stop her. During high school, she never lost a meet.

After triumphing in the 1956 Olympics, Wilma did even better in the 1960 Olympic Games. She won gold medals in the 100 meters, 200 meters, and 4 × 100 relay. She became the first American woman to win three gold medals in one Olympics.

"My mother taught me very early to believe I could achieve any accomplishment I wanted to," Wilma said. "The first was to walk without braces."

Also in the 1960 games, women were allowed to compete in the 800 meters for the first time. Four years later, the 400 meters was added for women.

Women's competition continued to grow. In the 1972 Olympics, the 1,500-meter and 4 × 400 meter relay joined the slate of women's events. In the 1984 games, the 400-meter hurdles and pentathlon came on board (later replaced by the heptathlon).

The newest event for women—pole vault—was introduced in the 2000 Olympics in Sydney. It's already produced superstars, such as Stacy Dragila, who won the first Olympic gold medal and holds the indoor and outdoor world records. With pole vaulting still in its infancy for women, there's plenty of opportunity for athletes to make their mark.

Today, women have achieved almost equal standing with men in track and field. In the 2000 games, for instance, women competed in 22 events, only two less than men.

More girls than ever are participating in track and field in high school. For instance, 415,677 girls across the country competed in the sport in the 2001–02 school year, according to the National Federation of State High School Associations. Track ranked behind only basketball in popularity, and well ahead of soccer, softball, and volleyball.

Girls continue to rewrite the record books. A look at past records shows how far they have come. In the 1952 Olympics, for instance, the winning time in the women's 100-meter dash was 11.5 seconds. Today, the high school record has far surpassed that—11.04 seconds. Likewise, the winning high jump in the 1952 Olympics was 5'5". Today, girls have cleared 6'4".

Fortunately, there's no shortage of role models in track for young athletes. Mary Decker is a good example. She began running when she was only 11 and two years later ran a remarkable 4:55 mile. She also set an age-group record in the 800 meters. When she was only 14, she competed against the feared Soviet Union team in Moscow in a televised event. She once nonchalantly said that she could beat most boys her age.

"I don't want to run with the boys," she said. "It's stupid."

Mary's running career lasted more than 25 years, a testament to her persistence and drive. She overcame countless injuries and surgeries to keep running when most others would have hung up their cleats. As an adult, she set several world records and competed in four Olympics, the first in 1984. Each time she was a favorite but disappointingly failed to win a medal. Still, she kept competing and is regarded as one of the greatest women track athletes of all time.

Jackie Joyner-Kersee, who won medals in the heptathlon in three Olympics, is another model of motivation. She, too, hasn't let obstacles get in her way. Jackie suffers from severe asthma.

"Some days, I'm just struggling to make it through," she said. "It wasn't until I nearly died from an attack that I began to take my condition seriously. I started to think of my asthma as part of my training, and I had to attack it with the same commitment and discipline."

She began setting goals for herself when her mother died suddenly. Jackie was only 18. Determined to succeed, she earned a basketball scholarship to the University of California at Los Angeles, one of the country's top athletic schools, and graduated on time.

Despite achieving fame, Jackie remains humble and keeps her achievements in perspective. She hasn't forgotten the true reason for participating in sports.

"The medals don't mean anything, and the glory doesn't last," she once said. "It's all about your happiness. The rewards are going to come, but the happiness is just loving the sport and having fun performing."

Another inspiring athlete is Gail Devers, a close friend of Jackie-Joyner Kersee. Today, Gail is hailed as one of the all-time great women sprinters. She won the gold medal in the 100 meters in the 1992 and 1996 Olympics and holds the U.S. record in the event. Her career has spanned more than a decade and is still going strong as she reaches her mid-30s, a ripe old age for sprinters.

People are surprised to learn that Gail's career almost ended before she achieved worldwide recognition. In 1988, she was diagnosed with Graves disease, a serious thyroid disorder. After a series of complications, her feet began to swell, blister, crack, and bleed. She couldn't walk and was told that her feet might have to be amputated.

Gail didn't despair. Doctors changed treatments, and she began a slow and painful recovery culminating in her success at the 1992 Olympics.

Many top sprinters are tall, but Gail has never let her short stature—she's 5'2"—deter her.

"I love the sport, and I want to continue to excel," she said. "I think my best is yet to come."

2
SPRINTS

When most people think of track, the first events that come to mind are sprints—the 100-, 200-, and 400-meter races.

People are fascinated with pure speed, and sprints showcase it. The performance of a winning sprinter carries the same aura and excitement as that of a home-run champ in baseball. Each delivers a sudden, explosive moment that propels them to the pinnacle of their respective sport. And each gets to take that self-satisfying "victory lap."

Some people are born with speed, some are not. Unfortunately, we can't dictate our genes. It takes natural-born talent—speed—to be a successful sprinter. However, someone blessed with adequate speed can improve dramatically with proper fundamentals and training.

Sprinters come in all shapes and sizes. Short, muscular athletes can excel. So can tall, lean ones. Don't look in the mirror and immediately decide you can't be a sprinter. You might be surprised. If you're willing to work hard and study the mechanics of sprinting, you can succeed.

Typically, athletes compete in only one or two of the sprinting events. It is rare to have the talent—and stamina—to compete in the 100, 200, and 400. The 400 meters is considered the most difficult because of its length. In the last 100 meters or so of the race, your body will cry out to stop. You must be mentally prepared to face the pain and keep going.

Years ago, the 400 meters was considered a middle-distance race. But with advanced knowledge and better training methods, today's runners must approach the event as a virtual all-out sprint. It's a grueling but rewarding event.

Before you begin training for any sprint, it's important to properly warm up and stretch. Think of your body as a finely tuned sports car. It can go very fast. But you wouldn't start a car and immediately floor it to reach top speed. No, you let the engine idle for a few seconds, then start out slowly before building speed.

The same should be true with your body. If you throw on your workout clothes and immediately run your hardest, you're likely to suffer an injury, often a pulled hamstring or other muscle. These are not major injuries, but they could keep you out of competition for several weeks. In high school, that could mean missing the heart of the season or the championship meet.

Injuries can normally be avoided with proper warm-up and stretching. A warm-up refers to a brief, low-intensity exercise, such as a short jog, that increases blood flow, heart rate, and body temperature. A proper warm-up gets your body ready for action. It should be the first step in a workout.

Next, you're ready for stretching exercises. These are done in a stationary position. They do not place demands on your heart or lungs. Instead, stretching makes your muscles more limber and increases your range of motion. Stretching is like tuning the strings on a piano or guitar. It lets your "instrument" (your body) produce the best results.

In Chapter 10, we list some suggested stretches. We group them into the three main categories: those for running, those for jumping, and those for throwing. Make a point of learning these stretches, or similar ones, and doing them faithfully. They only take a few minutes but can build a foundation for a successful and injury-free season.

In this chapter on sprinting—and in the following chapters—we begin with a brief section called The Basics that covers the rules and objective of an event. Next, we discuss proper technique. Then, we list common faults in technique along with ways to correct them. After that, we offer drills that will help reinforce proper form and a "feel" for the event. Lastly, each chapter concludes with sample workouts. They are divided into workouts for off-season, early season, and mid-season.

THE BASICS

- Sprinters run on a 400-meter oval track, divided into six or eight lanes.
- Modern tracks are made of all-weather synthetic rubber or polyurethane, instead of gravel or cinders, as in times past.
- Sprinters run counterclockwise, with their left arms toward the infield.
- Portable, metal starting blocks are used to help sprinters get a better takeoff. The blocks are adjustable to allow athletes to set varying distances between feet for a comfortable position.

- In the 200 and 400 meters, the starting blocks are staggered instead of being in a straight line because sprinters run on turns. If the blocks were lined up (as in the 100 meters), runners in the inside lanes would have an advantage by running a shorter distance.
- Most states allow no false starts—that is, taking off before the starter's pistol fires. If a runner does so, she is disqualified.
- Sprints are run in a series of qualifying "heats," or rounds. The runners with the fastest times advance to the final. Those with the best qualifying times run in the center lanes in the final.
- Athletes wear light shoes with a maximum of 11 cleats per shoe, each no more than 9 millimeters long. All the cleats are in the front of the shoe because sprinters' heels never touch the track.
- Runners in the 100, 200, and 400 meters must remain in their lanes throughout the race or they may be disqualified. (Athletes in the 800 meters are allowed to change lanes.) In addition, any runner who jostles or impedes another runner may be disqualified.
- The winner is the one whose torso—not any other part of the body—reaches the finish line first.
- The 400-meter race became an Olympic event for women in 1964, 16 years after the 200 meters was opened to women.

TECHNIQUE

Sprinting involves several elements: the start, acceleration, full stride, and finish. Each stage is critical. For instance, it's difficult to overcome a slow start to win a race. Likewise, a quick start is useless unless it's followed by brisk acceleration, powerful stride, and strong finish.

The Start

Starting technique has evolved more than any other element of sprinting. Many years ago, for instance, runners used a standing start. Later, starting blocks came into use, and sprinters adopted a kneeling position—feet against the blocks with one leg in front of the other, and the rear knee on the track. Today, all sprinters use a crouch start, although individual variations exist.

Some, for example, adjust the blocks so that their feet are close together. This is called a "bunched" start and is often used by sprinters with shorter legs. Other sprinters prefer more distance between their feet. This medium position is the most common. Runners with long legs sometimes place their feet far apart in the "elongated" position.

Sprinters must also decide which leg to place in the back block and which in front. Some coaches believe that a runner's stronger leg

Starting blocks with feet in bunched position

Starting blocks in medium position

should be in back because it takes an extra stride. Others think the stronger leg should be in front because it stays in contact longer with the starting block. There is no correct starting position for everyone.

Starting blocks in elongated position

For most people, there's a good way to tell which foot should be in back. Stand with your feet together and have someone gently push you from behind. One foot will naturally step forward to prevent you from falling. That foot should be in the back because it's the one you naturally step with first.

Sprinters should get used to the sounds that precede a race. A starter announces "on your marks," followed by a short pause and then "get set." He or she then fires a pistol into the air to signal the runners to take off.

When sprinters hear the first command ("on your marks") they get in their stances. Their weight should be equally divided between their back knee and outstretched fingers of both hands. Their fingers should be as close to the starting line as possible without touching it. Arms should be at least shoulder-width apart and pointing down at a 90-degree angle. The forward knee is even with or slightly behind the arms. Eyes remain focused on the ground 1–1.5 meters in front of the hands.

When sprinters hear "set," they stay in their crouch but raise their hips about 4 inches above their head. The front leg, as a result, bends about 90 degrees. The back leg is a little straighter at about 120 degrees. Both feet should be pressed firmly against the blocks. Sprinters then roll their shoulders slightly ahead of the fingers and lean toward the starting line. At this point, the athlete is like a powerfully coiled spring, ready for takeoff. Some runners take a deep breath and hold it, waiting for the starter's pistol.

When the gun is fired, runners explode out of the blocks, driving their legs and learning forward at a 45-degree angle for the first five or six meters. Staying down is very important. If a runner rises too quickly, she'll be unable to reach her maximum speed and will probably lose the race. During practice, some coaches emphasize the importance of staying down. They stand a few steps in front of the starting line and raise their arms to shoulder height. Sprinters must pass under their arms without ducking.

Just as driving the legs is important, so is pumping the arms. The two should work in harmony—fast arms usually mean fast legs. Arms should be bent at a 90-degree angle, and you should strive for full arm extension backward and forward. Imagine you're reaching for your back pocket, then your chin, over and over.

The 400 meters requires a slightly different start than the 100 and 200. First, the starting blocks should be angled toward the inside of the track because the race involves curves. Because the 400 is a longer event, runners don't explode as quickly out of the blocks. They pace themselves, building speed more gradually. Still, runners shouldn't dally near the starting blocks, thinking they'll save all their energy for the end. If they do, they'll fall too far behind and have no chance of winning.

The 400 meters, more than the other two sprints, requires strategy. It's almost—but not quite—a full sprint. Knowing your body's capacity and when to kick into a higher gear is critical.

On your marks position

Set position

Coming out of starting blocks

Acceleration

As a sprinter gains speed, her forward lean lessens and body becomes more upright. At the same time, her knees rise higher and higher toward her chest. Her stride lengthens. Her heels fly backward, almost touching her buttocks. Arms pump vigorously but smoothly. Your hands should rise to chest level but not cross an imaginary vertical center line on your chest. Don't let your arms fly wildly from side to side or they can twist your shoulders and cause you to veer. If you don't stay in the center of the lane, you're wasting motion and adding distance to the race.

The 100 meters is a straightaway, but sprinters in the 200 and 400 must navigate turns. During a turn, proper form is essential. Centrifugal force pulls you toward the outside of the lane and can cost you time. Place your right arm across your body slightly to help you hug the inside of the lane. Beginning sprinters, especially, must practice leaning toward the infield of the track to let them fully accelerate down the straightaway. Don't think the turns as a chance to relax. Attack them. Try to come out of turns in the lead and then maintain it.

Full Stride

Once a sprinter reaches full speed (usually at about 70 or 80 meters in the 100 meters), it's critical to maintain proper form to the finish line. Remember these points:

Upright sprinting position

- Keep an erect posture with only a slight forward lean.
- Run on the balls of your feet.
- Stay relaxed.
- Feel your rhythm develop.
- Keep your eyes on the finish line. Don't look back at competitors.

Finish

Often, sprinters unconsciously slow down near the finish line. They do this because of fatigue or because they're concentrating only on reaching the tape not running *through* it. Sprinters should visualize the finish line 10 meters past its actual point. This encourages you to maintain full speed to the end. Here's another critical point: Know the exact location of the finish line before you start. Sometimes, it's not obvious unless you look

Lean at finish line

first. Many races have been lost by athletes miscalculating the finish line.

Another common mistake is that athletes try to lengthen their stride toward the end, thinking it will create greater speed. However, the opposite is true. Longer, unnatural strides disrupt your rhythm and slow you down.

As sprinters reach the finish, they should lean forward slightly. A properly timed lean can provide the margin of victory at the tape. On the other hand, an improperly timed lean can cost you a race.

There are different types of leans. Some runners make a quick dip at the tape, ducking their head and torso. Others make an aggressive lunge—head down, arms pulled back, almost falling into the tape. Still others lunge and rotate one shoulder forward to try to gain an edge.

Experiment with different techniques to find one that feels comfortable.

RECORDS

100 Meters

WORLD RECORD

- 10.49 (Florence Griffith-Joyner—USA, 7/16/88)

U.S. NATIONAL RECORDS

- [ages 13–14]—11.74 (Joyce Alexis of Denver, Colorado, 7/6/97)
- [ages 15–16]—11.34 (Angela Williams of Ontario, California, 7/28/95)
- [ages 17–18]—11.10 (Michelle Glover of Pennsauken, New Jersey, 1980)

200 Meters

WORLD RECORD

- 21.34 (Florence Griffith-Joyner—USA, 9/29/88)

U.S. NATIONAL RECORDS

- [ages 13–14]—24.03 (Angela Williams of Ontario, California, 7/1/94)
- [ages 15–16]—23.26 (LaShauntea Moore of Akron, Ohio, 7/31/99)
- [ages 17–18]—23.32 (Monique Henderson of San Diego, California 7/27/00)

400 Meters

WORLD RECORD
- 47.60 (Marita Koch—East Germany, 10/6/85)

U.S. NATIONAL RECORDS
- [ages 13–14]—53.40 (Brandi Cross of Houston, Texas, 7/28/02)
- [ages 15–16]—52.11 (Stephanie Smith of Macon, Georgia, 7/29/01)
- [ages 17–18]—51.31 (Monique Henderson of San Diego, California, 7/27/00)

Source: USA Track & Field

FAULTS AND FIXES

No sprinter is perfect. Some struggle with mechanics more than others. But even the best sprinters can develop bad habits that hurt their performance.

It's up to a coach to spot imperfections. A trained eye can quickly assess a problem and correct it. Fixes may be easier than you think.

Below are some common problems, their causes, and ways to correct them.

Fault: In the set position, a sprinter's back stays parallel to the ground, instead of hips rising higher than the head.
Result: Prevents full acceleration out of the starting blocks.
Fix: Move blocks closer together. Focus eyes down, 1–1.5 meters ahead of hands, instead of at the finish line.

Fault: In the set position, a sprinter's shoulders remain behind the hands.
Result: Shifts the body's center of gravity to the rear, causing a sprinter to be off balance coming out of the blocks.
Fix: Move shoulders a few inches ahead of the hands. Adjust blocks if necessary.

Fault: Sprinter stands up too quickly out of the blocks.
Result: Reduces acceleration, makes first strides short and weak.
Fix: Stay low for the four or five meters. Focus on driving legs and arms vigorously. For practice, have someone stand in front of you with their arms extended then run under them.

Fault: Sprinter doesn't run in a straight line down the track.
Result: Prevents proper rhythm, creates wasted effort.
Fix: Relax arms, keep them close at your side, and pump them in parallel fashion. This prevent your body from twisting. Also, focus your eyes straight ahead at the finish line.

Fault: Sprinter leans slightly backward, instead of forward.
Result: Creates resistance, inhibits momentum.
Fix: Practice running in place. Then run backward a few meters, then run forward. This will give you the sensation of a proper forward lean.

She said it . . .
"Don't follow in anyone's footsteps. Make your own prints, because you are the future of tomorrow."

—Jackie Joyner-Kersee, Olympic gold medal winner in heptathlon.

DRILLS

To Improve Starts

- Practice getting in the "on your marks" position, then the "set" position. Come out of the starting blocks at half speed a few times, then three-quarters speed. Concentrate on proper form—body down, legs driving toward chest. As you learn to feel the correct technique during practice, you'll be able to explode out of the blocks without worrying about form.

To Improve Muscle Tone and Flexibility

- Stand erect with feet parallel at shoulder width. Gradually, take a big step forward with your right leg until your left knee touches the ground. Feel your leg muscles stretch. Hold the position for two or three seconds. Maintain your balance. Then lunge with your left leg until your right knee touches the ground. Hold. Repeat three or four times.
- Stand with feet parallel and almost touching. Hop forward five times on one leg. Swing arms forward and up simultaneously. Keep other knee at 90-degree angle. Stop. Gain your balance.

Lunges (above and right)

Hopping (above and right)

Hop forward five times on other leg. Swing arms. Do two or
three times.

- From a standing start, take a large leap forward with one leg.
  Touch down briefly. Push off with that foot, then leap with the
  other leg, driving arms forward and up. Proceed for 40 meters.
  Feel your "hang" time. Also feel the brief touch down and
  push off.

To Improve Acceleration and Build Endurance

- Find an area that has a slight incline of about 30 degrees. Run
  200 meters straight ahead at half speed, concentrating on
  proper sprinting form. Rest briefly. Repeat. Then run 200
  meters at three-quarters speed. Rest. Repeat. Finally, run 200
  meters at full speed. Feel the difference in your legs and upper
  body as you run faster.
- Jog a few meters straight ahead. Then, jump slightly and rotate
  180 degrees (facing the opposite direction). Touch down briefly
  with both feet, then sprint full speed for 20 meters, with proper
  body lean. Repeat three times.
- Sprint 50 meters on a track. Then jog 100 meters. Sprint 50
  meters, jog 100. Repeat four times.
- (*alternate*): Run 200 meters at 80 percent speed. Concentrate on
  proper sprinting form. Walk 100 meters. Again, run 200 meters
  at 80 percent. Maintain form. Walk 100 meters. Then run 200
  meters at 90 percent. Walk 100 meters. Then run 200 meters at
  full speed.

To Improve Stride Length and Consistency

- From a standing start, begin running at half speed, raising knees
  (in exaggerated fashion) to 90 degrees. Continue for 50 meters,
  with both knees reaching 90 degrees over and over. Concentrate
  on maintaining form more than building speed. Repeat.
- Begin running at half speed, kicking heels backward until they
  almost touch buttocks. Continue for 50 meters, kicking heels
  backward rhythmically. Maintain form. Don't worry about
  increasing speed. Repeat.
- Begin jogging. Leap forward with one leg (in exaggerated fashion),
  touch down briefly with foot and feel as if you're "pulling" the
  ground back toward and under your body. Proceed for 50 meters.
  Keep a slow pace and maintain form, feeling your body move
  forward as your feet pull the ground toward you. Repeat.
- Place 10 short sticks (about four inches high) in a straight line
  four feet apart. Stand behind the sticks and run directly over

them, avoiding contact. Emphasize high knee lift, brief touch down, and smooth stride. Rest briefly. Repeat twice.

Games to Liven Up Training

- Get two teams of three sprinters each. Stand behind a line. The first runners sprint to a cone 25 meters in front, circle around and sprint back to tag the next team member. (Allow sufficient space for both athletes to turn around). Repeat several times.
- Pair off athletes. Both begin running at the same time. The runner in front tries to shake off the other, weaving in and out of a large open space. The

Bounding (top row and above)

other runner tries to shadow her, staying within tagging distance. Reverse roles. Do for five minutes.

- Pair off with a partner. Using a wide strap or belt, one runner pulls the other like a horse pulling a cart. The partner holding the strap provides gentle resistance and stays in rhythm with the athlete in front. Gradually increase resistance so that the runner in front has to work harder and harder while maintaining good sprinting form. Proceed for 50 meters. Then reverse roles.

SUPERSTAR: FLORENCE GRIFFITH-JOYNER

Florence Griffith-Joyner had tremendous talent. She also had style.

She wore colorful, one-legged tights as she sped past her opponents. Her other trademarks were her long, flowing hair and loudly painted, six-inch nails.

"Looking good is almost as important as running well," she once said.

"FloJo," as she was nicknamed, set world records in the 100 and 200 meters in 1988, earning the title "World's Fastest Woman." Since then, no one has come close to breaking her records. Also in 1988, she won three gold medals in the Olympics (100, 200, and 4 × 100 relay) and one silver medal (4 × 400 relay). She became the first American woman to win four medals in any sport.

Florence overcame great odds to achieve her fame. She was one of 11 children raised by a single mother in a low-income housing project. She began running at age seven and became an instant phenomenon, beating all the girls she raced against and most of the boys. At 14, Florence won the Jesse Owens National Youth Games, named for a famous Olympic athlete.

She set records at her Los Angeles high school. After graduating in 1978, she attended California State University and the University of California at Los Angeles.

Florence first tried out for the Olympics in 1980 but failed. Undeterred, she qualified for the 1984 Olympics and won a silver medal in the 200 meters.

The best was yet to come. Four years later, she capped her career with her magnificent, four-medal performance in the 1988 Olympics. She was named the Associated Press Female Athlete of the Year and the Sullivan Award winner as the nation's outstanding amateur athlete.

(continued)

(continued)

"People don't pay much attention to you when you are second best," FloJo said at the time. "I wanted to see what it felt like to be number one."

A year later, she retired and achieved success in other fields. She became involved in modeling, writing, fashion design, and cosmetics. President Bill Clinton named her co-chair of the President's Council on Physical Fitness and Sports in 1993.

Tragically, FloJo lived only five more years. She died in her sleep of an apparent heart attack on September 21, 1998. She was only 38 years old.

The world mourned her death. President Clinton spoke for many people when he commented on her passing.

"We were dazzled by her speed, humbled by her talent, and captivated by her style," Clinton said. "Though she rose to the pinnacle of the world of sports, she never forgot where she came from."

SAMPLE WORKOUTS

100, 200 METERS (OFF-SEASON)	
Monday	Warm-up Stretching Sprint drills Five runs of 400–480 meters with six-minutes' rest at 50–60 percent of maximum Cooldown
Tuesday	Warm-up Stretching Sprint drills Eight 110-meter runs on a curve at 70–80 percent maximum Weights
Wednesday	Warm-up Stretching Sprint drills Five runs of 300–400 meters with six-minutes' rest at 60–70 percent of maximum Cooldown
Thursday	Warm-up Stretching Sprint drills

	Plyometrics (leaping exercises) and standing long jumps Cooldown Weights
Friday	Warm-up Stretching Sprint drills Five runs of 300–400 meters with six-minutes' rest at 60–70 percent of maximum Cooldown
Saturday/Sunday	Rest

100, 200 METERS (EARLY SEASON)

Monday	Warm-up Stretching Sprint drills Five runs of 300–400 meters with six-minutes' rest at 70–80 percent of maximum Cooldown
Tuesday	Warm-up Stretching Sprint drills Eight 110-meter runs on a curve at 70–80 percent of maximum Relay handoffs Weights
Wednesday	Warm-up Stretching Sprint drills Five runs of 200–300 meters with six-minutes' rest at 75–90 percent of maximum Cooldown
Thursday	Warm-up Stretching Sprint drills Relay handoffs Cooldown Weights
Friday	Warm-up Stretching Sprint drills Five runs of 300–400 meters with six-minutes' rest at 70–80 percent of maximum Cooldown
Saturday/Sunday	Rest

100, 200 METERS (MID-SEASON)	
Monday	Warm-up Stretching Sprint drills Five runs of 160–200 meters with six-minutes' rest at 85–100 percent of maximum Cooldown
Tuesday	Warm-up Stretching Sprint drills Starts Relay handoffs Cooldown Weights
Wednesday	Warm-up Stretching Sprint drills Five runs of 120–200 meters with six-minutes' rest at 85–100 percent of maximum Cooldown
Thursday	Warm-up Stretching Sprint drills Starts Relay handoffs Cooldown Weights (Upper body)
Friday	Competition or stretch and jog
Saturday	Competition or stretch and jog
Sunday	Rest

400 METERS (OFF-SEASON)	
Monday	Warm-up Stretching Sprint drills Five runs of 400–600 meters with six-minutes' rest at 50–70 percent of maximum Cooldown
Tuesday	Warm-up Stretching Sprint drills and plyometrics Eight 110-meter runs on a curve at 70–80 percent of maximum Weights

Wednesday	Warm-up
	Stretching
	Sprint drills
	Five runs of 400–600 meters with six-minutes' rest at 50–70 percent of maximum
	Cooldown
Thursday	Warm-up
	Stretching
	Sprint drills and plyometrics
	Eight 110-meter runs on a curve at 70–80 percent of maximum
	Weights
Friday	Warm-up
	Stretching
	Sprint drills
	Five runs of 400–600 meters with six-minutes' rest at 50–70 percent of maximum
	Cooldown
Saturday/Sunday	Rest

400 METERS (EARLY SEASON)

Monday	Warm-up
	Stretching
	Sprint drills
	Five runs of 300–500 meters with six-minutes' rest at 65–85 percent of maximum
	Cooldown
Tuesday	Warm-up
	Stretching
	Sprint drills
	4 × 400 relay exchanges
	Eight 110-meter runs on a curve at 70–80 percent of maximum
	Weights
Wednesday	Warm-up
	Stretching
	Sprint drills
	Five runs of 300–500 meters with six-minutes' rest at 65–85 percent of maximum
	Cooldown
Thursday	Warm-up
	Stretching
	Sprint drills
	4 × 400 relay exchanges

	400 METERS (EARLY SEASON) (*continued*)
	Eight 110s on a curve at 70–80 percent of maximum
	Weights
Friday	Warm-up
	Stretching
	Sprint drills
	Five runs of 400–600 meters with six-minutes' rest at 50–70 percent of maximum
	Cooldown
Saturday/Sunday	Rest

	400 METERS (MID-SEASON)
Monday	Warm-up
	Stretching
	Sprint drills
	Two to four runs of 300–400 meters with eight-minutes' rest at 85–100 percent of maximum
	Cooldown
Tuesday	Warm-up
	Stretching
	Sprint drills
	4 × 400 relay exchanges
	Five 110s on curve at 90–95 percent of maximum
	Weights
Wednesday	Warm-up
	Stretching
	Sprint drills
	Two to four runs of 300–400 meters with eight-minutes' rest at 85–100 percent of maximum
	Cooldown
Thursday	Warm-up
	Stretching
	Sprint drills
	4 × 400 relay exchanges
	Five 110s on curve at 90–95 percent of maximum
	Weights
Friday	Competition or stretch and jog
Saturday	Competition or stretch and jog
Sunday	Rest

INJURIES

Injuries, unfortunately, are part of every sport. Track is certainly no exception. Leg injuries, as you would expect, are the most common in sprints. These can range from mild cramps to ligament tears that require surgery. Runners most often experience hamstring pulls, tendonitis, and shin splints, injuries that are setbacks but are not usually serious.

It is critical to become attuned to your body and learn the difference between a simple ache and a potentially serious injury. You've probably heard the phrase, "No pain, no gain." That's partly true because you won't progress unless you exert yourself in training. However, that's far different from working out or competing when you're hurt. Doing so will only make your injury worse and keep you out of action longer.

Coaches and trainers can help you determine the seriousness of an injury and get the appropriate treatment. But you have to speak up and let them know you might be hurt. They are not mind readers. Do not ignore pain to try to impress the coach with your toughness and desire to compete. It is far better to tell your coach you *might* have an injury and then find out it is nothing serious rather than keep it to yourself and have it get worse and affect your performance. In that case, you're cheating yourself, your teammates, and your coach.

Injuries have different causes. Some can be traced to an insufficient warm up before a workout. Others can result from an athlete suddenly increasing the frequency, intensity, or duration of their workouts. Always remember, that training is good, but overtraining is worse than undertraining.

Do not forget about your shoes. Worn out shoes or the wrong shoes for your event can greatly increase stress on your legs and lead to injuries. Running on hard surfaces over and over instead of on a cushioned track or grass creates more pounding on your legs.

Every runner develops sore muscles, particularly early in the season. These aren't a cause for concern. Usually, if you ice and elevate your leg then do sensible workouts, the soreness will go away. More serious injuries are ones like sprains and stress fractures, tiny fractures that never heal because athletes do not rest enough.

Be aware of a few warning signs of serious injury. For instance, if you feel a sudden, stabbing pain or hear a snap or pop, get help immediately. These pains or sounds can indicate that you've broken a bone or torn a ligament or tendon. Also, get help if your joints feel unusually loose or you can't move a part of your body the way you're accustomed.

Most schools have trainers who can make a preliminary assessment of your injury. But you and your parents should see a private doctor if it appears to be serious.

It is rare to have an injury so serious that it requires surgery. But if you do need an operation, depending on its seriousness, you'll need to re-assess whether you should continue in track and field. If you decide to keep going, rehabilitation becomes critical. Athletes who don't properly rehab an injury are far more likely to suffer another injury. The result could be lifelong impairment. Your school trainer can help with rehabilitation, but you'll also want to consult a doctor or rehab specialist.

It's important to realize and accept that injuries do happen in track and field. But if you are smart and properly conditioned, your chances of injury go way down and your chances of enjoyment go way up.

She said it . . .
"When I was running, I had a sense of freedom, of running in the wind. When I ran, I felt like a butterfly."

—Wilma Rudolph, first American woman to win three Olympic gold medals in track and field.

SUPERSTAR: MARION JONES

Talk about an outstanding high school career. Marion Jones won the California state championship in the 100 and 200 meters *all four years* she was in high school (1990–93).

At the University of North Carolina, she continued her winning ways, earning nationwide recognition. She also proved that track stars can excel in other sports. Marion was a key member of the UNC women's basketball team that won the national championship in 1994.

In the 2000 Olympics, the world got to know Marion. She won three gold medals (100 and 200 and 4 × 400 relays) and two bronze medals (long jump and 4 × 100). In doing so, she became the first woman track athlete to win five medals in one Olympics.

Growing up, she was inspired by the achievements of Florence Griffith-Joyner and Jackie Joyner-Kersee. After watching both compete in the 1988 Olympics, Marion wrote on a school blackboard: "I want to be an Olympic champion."

Marion worked hard to make her dreams came true. Coaches and fellow athletes marveled at her drive and self-confidence.

"I know that I train harder than anyone else in the world," Marion once said. "I love getting to the finish line first. If you dedicate yourself to something, it's important to make sure and finish it off."

Today, she has earned the title "World's Fastest Woman," a distinction her role model, FloJo, once held. Marion's times in the 100 and 200 are second only to the world records set by FloJo.

Marion is far from being finished as an athlete. She says she wants to win more medals in the 2004 and 2008 Olympics, then retire. She's already making plans for life after track. Like FloJo, Marion has an interest in modeling. In 2001, she was featured on the covers of *Vogue* and *Ebony* magazines. Her height of 5'10" makes her a natural for modeling.

"I love what I do," Marion said of track. "When I step on the track, it is fun for me. When I've done my best, I get goose bumps. Nothing is hard when you love what you do."

3
HURDLES

Hurdling takes the challenge of sprinting a step further.

Not only do athletes have to run fast, they also have to successfully clear a series of obstacles without tripping and falling. In most high school meets, girls compete in the 100- and 300-meter hurdles. Sometimes, they run the 400 meters instead of the 300. The 100 and 400 have 10 hurdles, the 300 has eight.

Successful hurdlers must have three main qualities. First is speed. A girl may easily clear hurdles time and time again, but if she isn't fast enough to pull away from her opponents she won't win. Like sprinters, hurdlers must be blessed with an ability for speed that can't be taught. You must be born with it.

Second, top hurdlers must be coordinated. Hurdling is one of the most technically complex events in track and field. Athletes must carefully measure and rehearse their steps between hurdles to achieve maximum rhythm and speed. To clear a hurdle properly, they must jump the right height at the right time. If they jump too high, they'll expend too much effort and lose time. If they jump too low, they'll hit the hurdle. Naturally, that hurts your time and your body. To be your best, you have to pay attention to details such as leg bend and extension.

The third quality of champion hurdlers is dedication. An athlete may be fast and coordinated, but if she doesn't practice tirelessly she won't win consistently. This may mean getting up time and time again after you've hit the hurdle and fallen to the track. Eventually, you'll get the hang of it if you persevere. Nobody becomes a first-rate hurdler overnight.

Many hurdlers are tall and lean because that build tends to produce long strides. The longer your strides, the fewer steps you have to take between hurdles. In addition, it can be easier to get over hurdles.

However, don't get discouraged if you're not tall. Some world-class hurdlers hover around five feet tall. Gail Devers, who is 5'2", is a good example. She holds the U.S. record in the 100-meter hurdles and won the World Championships in the 100 in 1993, 1995, and 1999. Gail and other top hurdlers have overcome short stature with speed and jumping skill.

Hurdlers are usually versatile athletes. They often excel in other track events, such as sprints, relays, and long jump. Coaches love to have outstanding hurdlers because they can be the foundation for a winning team.

Hurdling technique has changed little in recent decades. There is a general consensus on what works and what doesn't. However, coaches have many different ways of teaching hurdling. It's a complex event, so there is more than one way to approach it. The result is what is important.

THE BASICS

- The 100- and 400-meter events have 10 hurdles.
- In the 100 meters, the hurdles are 8.5 meters apart and 33 inches high. They can be lower for younger athletes.
- In the 400 meters, hurdles are 35 meters apart and 30 inches high. They, too, can be lower for younger competitors.
- The 100 meters became a women's Olympic event in 1972. The corresponding men's event, by comparison, is 110 meters. The shorter distance was set for women because their strides are shorter than men's.
- The 400 meters was added in the Olympics for women in 1984. Men also run 400 meters.
- Hurdles are L-shaped with horizontal support bars that lie on the track, metal uprights and crosspieces made of wood or plastic.
- Shoes worn by hurdlers are similar to those of sprinters. However, cleats on hurdling shoes are shorter so that they don't get caught on the hurdles.
- Training for hurdling events is similar to training for sprints.
- Hurdlers must learn how many steps to take between hurdles to achieve maximum rhythm and speed.
- Runners have to stay in their lanes for the whole race.
- Athletes are not penalized for *unintentionally* knocking down a hurdle. However, they are disqualified if they make it fall on

purpose. Runners are not penalized for hitting the hurdle if it remains standing.

- Hurdlers are disqualified if either foot or leg passes to the side of a hurdle instead of directly over it.
- A top runner takes about three seconds longer to run a race with hurdles than the same distance without hurdles.

TECHNIQUE

Hurdling can be an intimidating event to learn. No one likes pain, and when you're starting out you're bound to hit your shins and ankles on hurdles. You'll probably fall down too. Hang in there. You'll improve faster than you think you can. Give yourself time to grasp the mechanics of hurdling. Patience is key.

Hurdlers begin the race in starting blocks in a crouched position, just like sprinters. For a review of starts, check Chapter 2.

Like sprinters, hurdlers explode out of the blocks and lean forward at first. But they straighten up more quickly in order to prepare for the first hurdle. In the 100 meters, most girls take eight steps before the initial hurdle, which is 13 meters from the starting line. After the first hurdle, athletes should take three steps between hurdles and clear them with the same leg. The other hurdles are 8.5 meters apart.

Approach to hurdle and going over with legs extended

Clearing hurdle (side view)

**When landing, right foot comes down
on ball of foot**

Early in training, runners should identify their lead leg—the one that goes over the hurdle first. Everyone is more comfortable with one leg than the other. To identify your lead leg, try this exercise: Stand with your legs together and have someone gently push you from behind. One leg will step forward to keep you from falling—that should be your lead leg. It should be in the back position of the starting blocks.

As you approach the first hurdle, don't hesitate or stutter step. Take your final step and plant your foot opposite your lead leg firmly. At the same time, lift your lead knee toward your chest and extend your lower leg horizontally over the hurdle. Your toes should point upward. Don't lock your knee. Initially, this may sound very mechanical, but you will learn to make one quick, fluid motion.

The goal is to barely clear the hurdle. If you leap too high, you'll lose time and disrupt your rhythm. You and your coach should experiment to find the proper distance in front of the hurdles to start your jump. Generally, girls should take off about five feet in front.

As you clear the hurdle, make sure your head is toward the front of your body to maintain your balance. The arm opposite your lead leg should swing forward to give you momentum to clear the hurdle. The hand should be even with your chest, but it shouldn't cross an imaginary vertical centerline on your chest. Your palms should face down.

During the jump, your hips and shoulders should remain square to the hurdle. When you get tired, you'll tend to twist your hips or shoulders. As your lead leg goes over the hurdle, your back leg should fully extend behind you. You should feel like you're "pulling" it over the hurdle. At the same time, bring your opposite arm forward with your hand chest-high.

On each jump, your lead leg should land on the ball of the foot, and your foot should be directly under your body. If your foot is too far in front or behind, you'll be off balance when you land. Most girls should land on their lead leg about three feet past the hurdle. Their trailing leg lands at about the same place.

Once both legs are down, you should drive aggressively toward the next hurdle, keeping your shoulders parallel and eyes forward. Concentrate on one hurdle at a time and do not pay attention to the runner in the next lane. It can be distracting if her arms are flying toward you, but remain focused and run your race.

Between hurdles, some runners like to count "1-2-3" to keep the proper pace. However, as you progress your strides should become so automatic that you don't have to count your steps.

After clearing the 10th hurdle in the 100 meters, you still have 10.5 meters to the finish line. This distance is where many races are won or lost. You must be in such good shape that you can make a final burst. Remember, hurdling is a sprinting event. You want to get to the finish line first, not necessarily to clear the hurdles in the prettiest manner.

If you hit a few hurdles and still finish first, that's okay. Always think of *sprinting* over hurdles, instead of jumping over them. Some young athletes get so worried about the mechanics of hurdling that they forget to run their hardest.

During practice, most coaches like to watch a hurdler from three angles: in front, behind, and on the side. These views allow him or her to spot technical problems that will hurt performance. Listen to your coach. It's much easier to catch and correct errors early rather than to try to fix them once they've become ingrained.

Sometimes, coaches use hurdles with soft tops for beginners. These are less painful to hit. Coaches may also put hurdles on grass to make falls easier to take. Some coaches have beginners walk over low hurdles at first to concentrating on proper form, not speed. Once an athlete is able to run full speed, she may practice with only two or three hurdles, then gradually work up to more.

Often, coaches move the hurdles close together at first so an athlete can easily take three steps between them. Once her stride becomes automatic, the coach will spread the hurdles to regular distance.

Because the 100 meters is run in a straight line, all the hurdles are parallel. But in the 300 and 400, some hurdles are placed on turns.

Some athletes find it more natural and more efficient to clear hurdles with their left leg first. If their right leg goes first, their trailing leg may pass to the side of the hurdle, instead of directly over it. This is a violation of the rules that results in disqualification. Practice and find out which leg should be your lead leg.

In the 400 meters, the first hurdle is 45 meters from the starting line. Most girls take 22–25 steps before the first hurdle. The next hurdles are 35, and top hurdlers take 15 steps between them.

A winning hurdler has to master a series of complex arm and leg movements. The result is speed, beauty, and grace.

RECORDS

(In some parts of the country, girls compete in the 300-meter hurdles. But USA Track & Field, the sport's governing body, does not keep records for that distance.)

100-Meter Hurdles

WORLD RECORD

- 12.21 (Yordanka Donkova—Bulgaria, 8/20/88)

U.S. NATIONAL RECORDS

- [ages 13–14]—14.01 (Domenique Manning of Rialto, California, 6/9/01)
- [ages 15–16]—13.81 (Yolanda Johnson of Denver, Colorado, 7/14/84)
- [ages 17–18]—13.39 (Virginia Ginnie Powell of Seattle, Washington, 7/29/01)

400-Meter Hurdles

WORLD RECORD

- 52.61 (Kim Batten—USA, 8/11/95)

U.S. NATIONAL RECORDS

- [ages 13–14]—*do not compete in this event*
- [ages 15–16]—58.84 (Talia Stewart of Richmond, California, 7/29/01)
- [ages 17–18]—57.94 (Tiffany Ross of Miami, Florida, 7/29/01)

Source: USA Track & Field

FAULTS AND FIXES

Fault: Approach to the first hurdle is uneven, and the number of steps varies.
Result: Prevents full acceleration and drive over the hurdle. The first hurdle sets the tempo of the race. If you don't get over it cleanly, your chances of winning diminish.
Fix: Learn the proper number of steps you should take. Mark a spot on the track five meters in front of the hurdle. Then take the hurdle away. Practice running to that spot until you hit it consistently with your takeoff foot. Then put the hurdle back and practice.

Fault: Taking off too far from the hurdle.
Result: Runner hits hurdle squarely.
Fix: With your coach's help, determine the exact spot to begin your jump each time. Rehearse over and over. As a training aid, put chalk on the bottom of your shoe to see how your steps vary.

Fault: Jumping too high.
Result: Wasted effort. Reduces speed and disrupts rhythm.
Fix: Take off further from the hurdle so you can make a more horizontal instead of vertical jump. Practice with lower hurdles until you perfect your jumping technique.

Fault: Locking knee as you go over the hurdle.
Result: Makes it harder to land properly.
Fix: Do not be so mechanical. Think of *sprinting* over the hurdles, not *jumping* over them. Remember, you don't run with locked knees.

Fault: Hitting trailing leg on hurdle repeatedly.
Result: Disrupts rhythm, may result in a fall.
Fix: Fully extend the trailing leg until it's parallel to the track, with the toe pointing up. When your front leg lands, think of "pulling" the trailing leg over the hurdle. Work on flexibility exercises for your hips and thighs to make this easier.

Fault: Off-balance landing and/or landing on heel.
Result: Prevents full acceleration between hurdles and development of proper stride pattern.
Fix: Keep hips and shoulders square (parallel to hurdle) as you approach and jump. Maintain proper body lean. As you go over a hurdle, extend your ankle forward with toes pointing down to the track to land on the ball of your foot.

Fault: Straightening up too quickly after landing.
Result: Runner decelerates, has to regain correct sprinting form with forward lean.

Fix: Start your jump further from the hurdle so you have a smoother, flatter clearance and landing. Drive your upper body and lead leg over the hurdle to maintain momentum.

Fault: Hitting too many hurdles late in the race.
Result: Slows down final sprint, reduces chances of winning.
Fix: Work on conditioning, flexibility, and focus. Tired runners let their mechanics slip. Fix your eyes on the next hurdle. Ignore the runner in the next lane. Achieve and maintain your rhythm.

> *She said it . . .*
> "You have to love what you're doing. I thought I could do whatever I tried to do. I would challenge myself to run a certain time in practice. It would be like a game."
>
> —Evelyn Ashford, member of five Olympic teams (1976–92), winner of four gold medals and one silver.

DRILLS

High-Stepping

Set eight hurdles four feet apart. (Use hurdles that are only two feet tall.) Slowly begin "marching" over the hurdles, raising your knees high in an exaggerated manner. Keep toes pointing up as you step over the hurdle.

Jogging

Again, set eight hurdles four feet apart. (Use slightly taller hurdles, about $2^{1}/_{2}$ feet). At half-speed, begin running over the hurdles. Concentrate on high knee action with lead leg and full extension backward with trailing leg. Move your arm rhythmically and keep your shoulders and hips square.

Wall Exercise

Stand about three feet from a wall and lean against it with your right hand. Imagine that your left leg is your trailing leg. Extend it fully behind you so that it's parallel to the ground. Then simulate "pulling" it over the hurdle, bending at the knee and touching down on the ball of your foot.

High-stepping (above and right)

Wall exercise (above and right)

Leading leg drills

Leading Leg Drill

Set up six hurdles the normal distance apart (8.5 meters). Use regulation-height hurdles. If your leading leg is your right one, stand on the left side of the first hurdle. Then begin running toward the next hurdle and clear it with only your right (lead) leg. Concentrate on proper form. Continue that way over the remaining hurdles. (If you lead with your left leg, start on the right side of the first hurdle and clear them with only your left leg.)

Trailing Leg Drill

Same as leading leg drill, except you're clearing the hurdles with only your trailing leg. If your left leg is your trailing leg, start on the right side of the first hurdle. If your right leg leads, reverse.

Chalk Drill

With your coach's help, draw chalk lines where you should take off and land. Try to hit those marks as you run through eight regulation hurdles set at normal distance.

Trailing leg drills

Add-Ons

(Once you've become proficient). Start with four hurdles over 100 yards. Run full speed and concentrate on proper form. Then add two more hurdles and repeat. Again, add two (to get to eight hurdles) and repeat. Finally, add two more and run them all.

Uphill Runs

Find a hill that has about a 20-degree incline. Practice running 200-yard sprints up the hill. This teaches proper body lean and drive. Builds leg strength and endurance.

Stair Hop

Hop up 10 stairs on one leg only. Repeat with other leg. Teaches proper push-off technique. Builds leg strength.

SAMPLE WORKOUTS

100-METER HURDLES (OFF-SEASON)	
Monday	Warm-up Stretching Drills Five runs of 400–480 meters with six-minutes' rest at 50–60 percent of maximum Cooldown
Tuesday	Warm-up Stretching Drills Eight 110-meter runs on a curve at 70–80 percent of maximum Weights
Wednesday	Warm-up Stretching Drills Five runs of 300–400 meters with six-minutes' rest at 60–70 percent of maximum Cooldown
Thursday	Warm-up Stretching Drills Practice starts to first hurdle Weights
Friday	Warm-up Stretching Drills Five runs of 300–400 meters with six-minutes' rest at 60–70 percent of maximum Cooldown
Saturday/Sunday	Rest

100-METER HURDLES (EARLY SEASON)	
Monday	Warm-up Stretching Drills Five runs of 300–400 meters with six-minutes' rest at 70–80 percent of maximum Cooldown
Tuesday	Warm-up Stretching

SUPERSTAR: GAIL DEVERS

Gail Devers is a world-class hurdler. She's also a world-class sprinter. In other words, she's got plenty of talent.

She won the gold medal in the 100 meter dash in the 1992 and 1996 Olympics. She also holds the U.S. record in the 100 meter hurdles.

Gail's achievements are even more amazing when you consider that her career almost ended before her first Olympics. She was diagnosed with Graves disease, a serious thyroid disorder that caused her to experience a number of alarming symptoms: weight fluctuation, memory loss, headaches, excessive bleeding, and temporary blindness in one eye.

Doctors tried to treat the disease with radiation, but it made her condition worse. The radiation caused her feet to swell, blister, and crack, resulting in excruciating pain. Gail was told she might have to have both feet amputated. Fortunately, a change in treatment produced quick improvement, and Gail began a steady recovery.

100-METER HURDLES (EARLY SEASON) *(continued)*	
	Drills
	Eight 110s on a curve at 70–80 percent of maximum
	Relay handoffs
	Weights
Wednesday	Warm-up
	Stretching
	Drills
	Five runs of 200–300 meters with six-minutes' rest at 75–90 percent of maximum
	Cooldown
Thursday	Warm-up
	Stretching
	Drills
	Relay handoffs
	Cooldown
	Weights
Friday	Warm-up
	Stretching
	Drills
	Five runs of 300–400 meters with six-minutes' rest at 70–80 percent of maximum
	Cooldown
Saturday/Sunday	Rest

She went from being unable to walk, to walking gingerly in socks, to jogging, to returning to full competition. In 1991, she took the silver medal at the World Championships, followed by the gold in the 1992 Olympics, capping a remarkable comeback.

"The word 'quit' has never been part of my vocabulary," Gail once said. "I feel like I have a guardian angel looking over me."

She holds the U.S. record in the 100 meter hurdles—12.21, set in July 2000. At the time, she was 33 years old, much older than most record-setters in track. She attributes her longevity to proper training and focus.

Gail has used her success on the track to make positive changes in society. She's involved in a national campaign to increase awareness of thyroid disease, and she has established the Gail Devers Foundation to promote education, health, and athletic participation among youth.

"I realize I have been truly blessed," she said. "Now I want to share my good fortune by passing it on and helping others."

100-METER HURDLES (MID-SEASON)

Monday	Warm-up
	Stretching
	Drills
	Five runs of 160–200 meters with six-minutes' rest at 85–100 percent of maximum
	Cooldown
Tuesday	Warm-up
	Stretching
	Drills
	Starts
	Relay handoffs
	Cooldown
	Weights
Wednesday	Warm-up
	Stretching
	Drills
	Five runs of 120–200 meters with six-minutes' rest at 85–100 percent of maximum
	Cooldown
Thursday	Warm-up
	Stretching
	Drills
	Starts

100-METER HURDLES (MID-SEASON) *(continued)*

	Relay handoffs Cooldown Weights (upper body)
Friday	Competition or stretch and jog
Saturday	Competition or stretch and jog
Sunday	Rest

400-METER HURDLES (OFF-SEASON)

Monday	Warm-up Stretching Drills Five runs of 400–600 meters with six-minutes' rest at 50–70 percent of maximum Cooldown
Tuesday	Warm-up Stretching Drills and plyometrics Eight 110s on a curve at 70–80 percent of maximum Weights
Wednesday	Warm-up Stretching Drills Five runs of 400–600 meters with six-minutes' rest at 50–70 percent of maximum Cooldown
Thursday	Warm-up Stretching Drills and plyometrics Eight 110s on a curve at 70–80 percent of maximum Weights
Friday	Warm-up Stretching Drills Five runs of 400–600 meters with six-minutes' rest at 50–70 percent of maximum Cooldown
Saturday/Sunday	Rest

400-METER HURDLES (EARLY SEASON)

Monday	Warm-up Stretching Drills

	Five runs of 300–500 meters with six-minutes' rest at 65–85 percent of maximum Cooldown
Tuesday	Warm-up Stretching Drills 4 × 400 relay exchanges Eight 110s on a curve at 70–80 percent of maximum Weights
Wednesday	Warm-up Stretching Drills Five runs of 300–500 meters with six-minutes' rest at 65–85 percent of maximum Cooldown
Thursday	Warm-up Stretching Drills 4 × 400 relay exchanges Eight 110s on a curve at 70–80 percent of maximum Weights
Friday	Warm-up Stretching Drills Five runs of 300–500 meters with six-minutes' rest at 65–85 percent of maximum Cooldown
Saturday/Sunday	Rest

400-METER HURDLES (MID-SEASON)

Monday	Warm-up Stretching Drills Two to four runs of 300–400 meters with eight-minutes' rest at 85–100 percent of maximum Cooldown
Tuesday	Warm-up Stretching Drills 4 × 400 relay exchanges Five 110s on a curve at 90–95 percent of maximum Weights
Wednesday	Warm-up Stretching Drills

400 METER HURDLES (MID-SEASON) *(continued)*	
	Two to four runs of 300–400 meters with eight-minutes' rest at 85–100 percent of maximum
	Cooldown
Thursday	Warm-up
	Stretching
	Drills
	4 × 400 relay exchanges
	Five 110s on a curve at 90–95 percent of maximum
	Weights
Friday	Competition or stretch and jog
Saturday	Competition or stretch and jog
Sunday	Rest

She said it . . .

"I always had the knowledge and the faith within me that I could be the best. Running is something I wanted to do. No one was going to tell me I couldn't."

—Inger Miller, gold medal winner in 1996 Olympics in the 4 × 100 meter relay.

SUPERSTAR: KIM BATTEN

Kim Batten is proof that some athletes don't discover their best event immediately.

In high school, she excelled in the long jump. When she got to Florida State University in 1988, she found that her real talent was in the 400-meter hurdles.

In 1991, she won first place in the U.S. Championships and repeated the accomplishment *every year* from 1994 to 1998. She still holds the world record in the 400-meter hurdles—52.61, set in 1995.

Kim won a silver medal in the 1996 Olympics but failed to win a medal in the 2000 Olympics. A foot injury hindered her training leading up to the games.

After the Olympics, she became an assistant track coach at Florida State, her alma mater. Like many first-rate athletes before her, she decided to pass on her expertise to a younger generation.

"As a world champion and a world record holder, Kim brings a very unique perspective to the job," FSU head track coach Terry Long said when Kim was named to the staff. "This is a great opportunity for our athletes to learn from her."

4
MIDDLE-DISTANCE AND LONG-DISTANCE RACES

In middle- and long-distance races, the mind is as important as the body.

The 800, 1,500 meters (middle-distance), and the 3,000 (long-distance) require extreme mental toughness to overcome fatigue late in the race. These events also demand intelligence and pace judgment. They are unlike sprints, which call for a burst of speed and are over quickly. In middle- and long-distance races, athletes have to carefully expend their energy, running hard enough to stay in the competition, but saving enough energy to make a final "kick." They have to learn their bodies' limits.

In the 800-, 1,500-, and 3,000-meter races, the body and mind must work together. At times, they may give you conflicting messages. In the final meters of a close race, your body may say, "I want to quit. I'm out of gas." But your mind must override the body and press on to the finish.

Strategy is vital. For instance, you must always be aware of your position on the track in relation to others. You don't want to get "boxed in," stuck in a pack and unable to break free when you need to. Also, watch out for runners who take an early lead to try to coax others to stay with them. They are trying to wear you out.

As the race progresses, it's okay to be a few spots off the lead. In fact, many coaches say that's preferable because you do not have as much wind resistance as the lead runner. But you don't want to get too far behind. You may have a great kick, but it won't help if you're half a lap behind.

Top athletes in middle- and long-distance races are often specialists. They may not have the speed to run the 100 meters, and they might not have the endurance to run cross-country. But they have better-than-average speed and better-than-average endurance combined with tenacity and intelligence.

Sprinters, in comparison, can sometimes get by on talent alone. They may be naturally so fast that they don't have to train very hard. This isn't true for middle- and long-distance runners. The winners are usually the ones who work the hardest in practice. You have to run lap after lap, mile after mile. When you learn to face exhaustion in practice, and keep going, you'll be able to do the same at a meet.

The best athletes in middle- and long-distance races aren't casual about running. They must *love* to run. They must be willing, at times, to get out of bed before sunrise to train or to stay long after the sun sets. Some people even say there is a spiritual component to distance running. You must feel an inner *need* to run. It gives you a satisfaction like nothing else.

Do not be scared off by the demands of the 800-, 1,500-, and 3,000-meter distances. Training should be intense, but also fun at least part of the time. The real fun comes when you do your best in a meet. If your best keeps improving, you'll likely be a winner.

THE BASICS

- The 800-meter race evolved from the half-mile (805 meters). Some still refer to the 800 meters as the half-mile. The 1,500 is the metric equivalent of the mile (1,609 meters).
- The 800 meters was added as an Olympic event for women in 1960. The 1,500 became a women's Olympic event in 1972. The 3,000 is strictly a youth and high school event. At the college level and in the Olympics, athletes run 5,000 meters.
- In the 800, 1,500, and 3,000, runners do not use starting blocks. Instead, they stand and start in staggered position so that athletes in the inside lanes don't have an advantage.
- In the 800 meters, runners must stay in their lanes for the first turn (100 meters), then they can break toward the inside of the track. In the 1,500, and 3,000, runners can get out of their lanes immediately.
- Strategy is involved in all three distances. Sometimes, runners intentionally follow closely behind the frontrunner to benefit from less wind resistance.
- The key is pacing. You must stay close to the lead throughout the race and then have enough energy to sprint to the finish.

TECHNIQUE

Running technique differs a little for every event.

In sprints, for instance, runners burst out of the starting blocks with a sharp forward lean. They drive their legs and arms as fast as they can.

In middle- and long-distance races, runners start at a much slower pace, and their bodies are more upright. But don't think they're off on a leisurely jog. From the start, runners must work hard to jockey for position and plot their race.

To achieve your best time, you must learn the mechanics of running the middle- and long-distance races. For one thing, your strides are shorter. Your knees don't rise as high in front of you, and your heels don't kick up as much behind you as in sprints. These shorter strides let you maintain a steady rhythm—a key to success.

In the 800 meters, you should land on the balls of your feet. Your feet then become flat for a second, before you push off again with the balls of your feet. In the 1,500 and 3,000, you land nearly flat-footed, then push off.

Arm movements in the 800 are also slightly different than in the 1,500 and 3,000. In the 800, your arms swing forward chest-high, without crossing the center of your chest. In the two longer distances, your arms don't go as high and stay closer to your hips.

The middle- and long-distance races have one thing in common with sprints: Runners must keep their hips and shoulders square to the finish line. If you twist back and forth, you'll lose momentum and,

Landing position for 800 meters, on ball of foot

Landing position for 1,500 and 3,000 meters, almost flat-footed

consequently, time. Likewise, your body shouldn't move up and down a great deal. Steady and smooth is best.

The last quarter of these races (for instance, the final 200 meters in the 800-meter event) is the most important. You need to be close to the lead as you come out of the final turn and head into the straightaway. Then, you can shift into high gear and, you hope, blow past everyone else. In the ideal strategy you stay close, then strike.

Runners often begin their kick too soon. They may pass several runners and look like they're in great shape, heading to victory. Then, they simply run out of gas. Others pass them as if they're in slow motion. Learn to time your kick properly. This requires a lot of training. Determination is great, but if your body has nothing left, you're not going to win.

Some coaches say that runners should save 40 percent of their energy for the last quarter of the race. That's only an estimate, but it's a good rule of thumb. Of course, you can hold back too much. Then the greatest kick in the world won't do you any good.

Be sure to stay alert during the whole race. Watch out for someone who might suddenly cut in front of you or bump you. If you're not careful, you could fall and have no chance to win.

As you prepare for a race, consider the weather. If the track is wet, ask yourself if you will need to adjust your pace and perhaps start out slower to test your footing. Will you have the traction to make an all-out sprint at the end? Sometimes adverse conditions can throw off even top runners.

Here's another possibility. At a meet, the events before yours may run long. That leaves you with a lengthy delay. Your body may get stiff, and you may lose your mental focus. Before the race, realize that you may not run when you're scheduled. Be ready to adjust physically and mentally.

Finally, try to be aware of the opponents you will face. Find out if your main competitors, for instance, start fast or have a killer kick at the end. Track involves strategy. You must run your race while also being prepared for what others may do.

In middle- and long-distance races, the prize often goes to the smartest competitor.

RECORDS

800 Meters

WORLD RECORD

- 1:53.28 (Jarmil Kratochvilova—Czechoslovakia, 7/26/83)

U.S. NATIONAL RECORDS

- [ages 13–14]—2:09 (Treani Swain of Los Angeles, California, 8/1/98)
- [ages 15–16]—2:08.94 (Trisha Nickoley of Tecumseh, Kansas, 7/6/02)
- [ages 17–18]—2:07.05 (Tamieka Grizzle of Bronx, New York, 7/1/94)

1,500 Meters

WORLD RECORD

- 3:50.46 (Qu Yunxia—China, 9/11/93)

U.S. NATIONAL RECORDS

- [ages 13–14]—4:36.9 (Rebecca Mitchell of Geneva, Illinois, 7/27/96)
- [ages 15–16]—4:25.57 (Suzy Favor of Stevens Point, Wisconsin, 7/22/84)
- [ages 17–18]—4:26.39 (Cecilia Hopp of Cos Cob, Connecticut, 8/2/81)

3,000 Meters

WORLD RECORD

- 8:06.11 (Wang Junxia—China, 9/13/93)

U.S. NATIONAL RECORDS

- [ages 13–14]—9:57.16 (Deresa Walters of Rochester, New York, 7/4/87)
- [ages 15–16]—10:00.2 (Lisa Dressel of Colbert, Washington, 7/18/86)
- [ages 17–18]—9:37.24 (Dana Boyle of Carbondale, Colorado, 7/30/98)

Source: USA Track & Field

FAULTS AND FIXES

Fault: Runner has uneven, rough stride.
Result: Wastes energy, prevents proper rhythm.
Fix: Improve mechanics. Work on shorter, more consistent strides. Make sure you land on the balls of your feet (for 800 meters) or nearly flat-footed (for 1,500 and 3,000). Arms should swing smoothly.

Fault: Runner's torso twists from side to side.
Result: Never develops optimum pace.
Fix: Keep shoulders and hips square, eyes focused 50–100 meters down the track. As fatigue sets in, runners tend to twist. Be aware of this and combat it.

Fault: Runner appears tense, stiff.
Result: Expends too much energy.
Fix: Work on mechanics. Athlete may be unsure how the proper pace feels. Runner may be worried about having enough energy to finish, which is causing her to become tense.

Fault: Athlete insists on keeping up with the early leader.
Result: Poor pace management, runner uses too much energy at first, can't make strong kick at end.
Fix: Think about strategy. Realize that a race requires mental, as well as physical, preparation. Have someone videotape you during a meet to see the results of an improper pace.

Fault: Repeatedly getting "boxed in."
Result: Unable to pick up speed when you want, allowing others to dictate the race.
Fix: Pay more attention to competitors and your position on the track. Think about where you need to be to be able to make a charge.

Fault: Athlete consistently starts kick too soon.
Result: Runs out of energy before the finish, unable to retain lead.
Fix: Work on pace management, strategy. Learn your body's limits and how much energy you must conserve early to make a strong finish.

Fault: Runner leans backward, lets head roll around.
Result: Increases effort, inhibits rhythm.
Fix: Keep posture erect, torso slightly forward. Increase upper body strength through weight lifting and flexibility exercises.

Fault: Poor work ethic, dislikes training.
Result: No chance of winning.
Fix: Find another event or another sport.

She said it . . .
"I see myself as an artist. Running is the way I express my talent. I wish I could paint or write music, but running is what I do, and I feel great joy from it."

—Joan Nesbit, national indoor champion
in 3,000 meters in 1996.

DRILLS

Pace Practice

Place flags or cones at 50-meter intervals around a 400-meter track. Athletes must maintain a set pace (such as 15 seconds for 50 meters) to arrive at the marker when the coach's whistle blows. Repeat six times.

Time Travel

Athletes run different distances in the same time period, for instance, 50, 60, and 70 meters in 20 seconds each. Repeat each of those distances three times.

Interval Sprints

Run 50 meters at close to maximum speed, then walk 50 meters. Repeat. Run 75 meters at same speed, then walk 75 meters. Repeat. Finally, run 100 meters the same way, walk 100 meters and repeat.

Pyramid Sprints

(For all distances run at 75 percent of capacity.) Run 100 meters. Rest 15 seconds. Run 150 meters. Rest 15 seconds. Run 200 meters. Rest. (This is the top of the "pyramid," then starting working down to shorter distances.) Run 150 meters. Rest. Then 100 meters.

Cross-Country Training

Run continuously over a set course for 30 minutes to an hour, preferably one with hills and varied terrain. Under a coach's instruction, alternate between jogging, striding, and sprinting. May also mix in walking.

Uphill Runs

Find a hill with about a 20-degree incline. Run 200 yards up the hill. Rest 30 seconds. Run the same length down the hill. Repeat twice—up the hill, rest, down the hill, etc.

Hurdle Hops

Set five regulation hurdles on a track four yards apart. With both legs together, hop over the first hurdle, land, hop over the next one, etc., until you reach the end. Repeat.

Two-legged hurdle hops

Underwater Running

Find a pool. Get in about five feet of water and run sprints of 50 meters. Rest 30 seconds after each one. Do eight sprints. The water provides excellent resistance and helps build leg strength.

SAMPLE WORKOUTS

800, 1,500, 3,000 METERS (OFF-SEASON)	
Monday	Stretch
	Jog half-mile
	Do 30 minutes of road work
	Stretch
Tuesday	Stretch
	Jog half-mile

	Two to four 800-meter runs at 75 percent of maximum. Rest three minutes between each Weights
Wednesday	Stretch Jog half-mile Do 30 minutes of road work Stretch
Thursday	Stretch Jog half-mile Two to four 800-meter runs at 75 percent of maximum. Rest three minutes between each Weights
Friday	Jog half-mile Do 30 minutes of road work Stretch
Saturday	Compete in cross-country meet (many athletes take part in the fall cross-country season to prepare for the spring track season) or one-hour run
Sunday	Rest

800, 1,500, 3,000 METERS (EARLY SEASON)

Monday	Jog half-mile warm-up Stretch Two sets of 6–10 400-meter runs at 75–90 percent of maximum. Rest six minutes between sets Run 6–10 800s at 75–90 percent of maximum. Rest four minutes between sets Cooldown
Tuesday	Stretch One-hour run Weights
Wednesday	Jog half-mile warm-up Stretch Two sets of 6–10 400-meter runs at 75–90 percent of maximum. Rest six minutes between sets Run 6–10 800s at 75–90 percent of maximum. Rest four minutes between sets Cooldown
Thursday	Stretch One-hour run Weights
Friday	Competition or jog lightly
Saturday	Competition or jog lightly
Sunday	One-hour run

800, 1,500, 3,000 METERS (MID-SEASON)	
Monday	Jog half-mile warm-up Stretch Three to four 600-meter runs at 85–100 percent of maximum. Run one every 10 minutes Two sets of 8–12 400-meter runs at 75–90 percent of maximum. Run one every three minutes. Rest six minutes between sets
Tuesday	Stretch Jog half-mile Practice starts on a curve One-hour run Weights
Wednesday	Jog half-mile warm-up Stretch Three to four 600-meter runs at 85–100 percent of maximum. Run one every 10 minutes Two sets of 8–12 400-meter runs at 75–90 percent of maximum. Run one every three minutes. Rest six minutes between sets
Thursday	Stretch Jog half-mile Practice starts on a curve One-hour run Weights
Friday	Jog or competition
Saturday	Jog or competition One-hour run on Sunday
Sunday	One-hour run

She said it . . .
"All you have to do is believe in yourself—have a goal."

—Joetta Clark-Diggs, four-time Olympian (2000, 1996, 1992, 1988)
in the 800 and 1,500 meters.

SUPERSTARS: MARY DECKER AND ZOLA BUDD

Mary Decker and Zola Budd had outstanding track careers over many years.

But most people remember one moment in their careers: their collision during the 3,000 meters in the 1984 Olympics.

Mary, the favorite, fell to the track halfway through the event after colliding with Zola. Mary was closing in on the lead when she tripped over Zola's right heel and fell to the track. Zola, a 17-year-old who ran barefooted, was cut deeply by Mary's spikes. She appeared so shaken by the collision that she finished seventh, amid boos from spectators. Neither achieved their dream of an Olympic medal.

Mary initially accused Zola of intentionally running into her. Zola denied that. Spectators and track experts were divided on who was at fault or whether it was simply an unfortunate accident. A now-famous photo of Mary ran in newspapers around the world. She lay on the ground in pain and in tears, clutching her left thigh. She had to be carried from the track.

Leading up to the Olympics, both Mary and Zola appeared to be peaking. Mary had already been a top runner for more than a decade and had set seven world records. She missed out on the 1976 Games because of an injury. And in 1980, the United States and many other countries boycotted the Olympics in protest of the Soviet Union's invasion of Afghanistan. The 1984 Olympics were supposed to be Mary's time to shine.

Zola was just starting to make a name for herself. Earlier in 1984, she had broken Mary's world record in the 5,000 meters. Zola was from South Africa but represented Great Britain in the 1984 Games. Her unique barefoot running style became her trademark. She, too, was a top medal contender heading into the 1984 Olympics.

At the end of the race, after the heartbreaking collision, Zola tried to talk to Mary.

"I went up to apologize, but she said, 'Don't bother!'" Zola wrote in her autobiography.

Mary's disappointment subsided, and she continued to win races. In 1985, she set a world indoor record in the 2,000 meters and a world outdoor record in the mile.

Zola also did well. She continued to compete for Britain, winning the European title in the 3,000 meters in 1985, and

(continued)

(continued)

setting a world record in the 5,000 meters the same year. In addition, she won the world championship in cross-country in 1985 and 1986. In 1988, she returned to her native South Africa and finished her career, although her best days were over. Today, she lives on a farm in South Africa with her mother, husband, and three children.

"I'll never stop running." she said. "But it's not my whole life these days."

Mary, meanwhile, continued to pursue her Olympic dream after Zola's career had tailed off. In the 1988 Olympics. Mary entered as a favorite in the 3,000 meters but finished a disappointing 10th. In 1992, she failed to qualify for the Olympics, but she rebounded and made the U.S. team in 1996, although she failed to win a medal.

Mary remains one of greatest women runners of all time. She set a remarkable 17 world records and 36 U.S. records. Now in her mid-40s, she still competes occasionally, despite more than two dozen operations on her legs, feet and ankles.

Unfortunately, she has no realistic chance of achieving her dream of an Olympic medal. Still, she doesn't dwell on the disappointment. She's proud of her accomplishments and still enjoys running.

"I was born to run," she said. "I simply love to run. I don't feel complete without running."

5
RELAYS

Track is often thought of as an individual sport. But relays epitomize team effort.

Your relay team may have the four fastest girls in the state, but if they cannot work together and pass off the baton smoothly, their speed is useless. Teams with slower runners often win because they've mastered the baton exchange.

The most common relays are the 4 × 100 and 4 × 400, but meets may also include the 4 × 200 and 4 × 800. For each, proper coaching and training pay off in a big way. There are several acceptable ways to exchange the baton between runners and many unacceptable ways. The handoff should be practiced until it's perfected. This may seem dull and unnecessary to some. After all, how difficult could it be to hand a little baton to someone?

As it turns out, very difficult. During the pressure of a close race, handing off the baton smoothly can seem like a monumental achievement. Remember, both girls aren't standing still. That would be easy. No, both athletes should be running at, or close to, full speed. Plus, in the 4 × 100, the girl receiving the baton shouldn't look back to see it hit her hand. That costs valuable milliseconds.

Now, you can see why the handoff can be so tricky and require so much practice.

Sometimes, athletes receiving the baton can take off before they get full control of it. Then they drop the baton—a full-scale disaster. There's nothing worse than seeing the baton bounce around the track while your competitors pass you by. If you drop the baton, your chances of winning go way down. But still, don't quit. Occasionally, teams recover from a dropped baton and still win the relay. Keep in mind that the team in front may drop their baton too before the race is over. A dropped baton tests your mental stamina.

Relays are exciting to run and to watch. They require speed, timing, and coordination. You might assume that the coach would pick the four fastest girls for the relay team. That's not always the case. For instance, the girls must get along, and egos have to take a back seat. A lot of girls would like to run the final, anchor leg, and sprint across the finish line with the baton.

Only one person can be the anchor and the other three legs, actually, are just as important. If the first athlete doesn't have a strong run, the team may get so far behind that it's almost impossible to catch up. Likewise, if the second or third runners don't do well, even the speediest anchor won't rally the team.

Coaches must evaluate their runners carefully. They ask themselves a lot of questions in picking their team. Who has the best start? Who has the best finish? Who runs the best on turns? Who passes the baton best, who receives it best? For instance, the first runner only passes the baton, while the last runner only receives it.

In addition, some girls are fast, but they don't run well with a baton. A coach doesn't want that athlete on the track then, even though she may be great in individual sprints. Another consideration in putting together a team is the height of the runners. It's very difficult for a girl who is 5'10" to pass a baton smoothly to a girl who is 5'1". The taller girl has to reach down too far to hand it off, and the shorter girl has to reach up too much to grab the baton.

Relays can make or break a team's chances of winning a meet because they usually count more points than individual events. So your team members can do only so-so in individual events, yet the team can still win the meet if the relay team shines.

You see, track *is* a team sport.

THE BASICS

- The baton is a hollow tube made of metal, plastic, or wood. It can't be longer than 30 centimeters or weigh more than 50 grams.
- All relays have four runners.
- In the 4 × 100 relay, the baton handoff must occur within a 20-meter exchange zone. The zone starts 10 meters before the 100-, 200- and 300-meter lines, and it ends 10 meters beyond them. If the exchange is outside the zone, the team is disqualified.
- In the 4 × 100, the runner receiving the baton is allowed to begin running 10 meters before the start of the exchange zone.

This allows her to get a running start before she receives the baton.

- In the 4 × 100, team members must stay in their lanes for the whole race.
- In the 4 × 400, only the first lap and the first turn of the second lap are run in lanes. Then runners can break for the inside of the track.
- In the 4 × 400 relay, there is no "run-up" area before the exchange zone.
- After a runner passes the baton, she must stay in her lane until other runners have passed so she won't get in their way.

TECHNIQUE

The baton handoff is the most critical part of the relays. Many of the basic sprinting techniques apply to the race: powerful leg and arm movement, body lean, square shoulders.

But without a smooth exchange, your team probably won't win. The handoff should take place with both athletes running hard. It should be so fluid that it's hard to tell from the stands when the baton changed hands.

Two primary exchange styles are used: the upsweep and the downsweep. Both methods have advantages and disadvantages. Some coaches prefer one over the other based on the habits of their runners and the length of the race.

Whichever is used, runners should become so comfortable with it that it's almost automatic during a meet. If you have to think about how to position their hands and feet as the incoming runner approaches, you're much more likely to fumble the exchange and lose precious time. So, be prepared to practice the baton handoff over and over. You'll be glad you did.

Upsweep

This is the oldest method of handing off the baton. The runner receiving it reaches back with one arm and points her hand down at a 45-degree angle to the track. She forms a V with her thumb and forefinger.

The incoming runner places then places the baton firmly in her hand in an upward, sweeping motion. This is a "blind pass." The outgoing runner doesn't turn to look at the other runner or the baton. Proper timing is essential. The incoming runner shouts when she's getting close. Both runners must know exactly where to position their hands for a smooth exchange.

The upsweep technique is normally used in the 100-meter relay. Because it's a short event, the 100 demands a fast handoff to avoid losing even a fraction of second. Turning to look at the incoming runner wastes time.

However, there are several disadvantages to the upsweep. One, it's risky. If the two runners haven't rehearsed over and over, they're unlikely to make a smooth "blind" exchange. Second, the runners have to be close together to perform this handoff, and that increases the chance of a collision and a dropped baton. Third, the receiver's hand is pointing down, so it's easier to drop the baton during the exchange.

It's critical that the outgoing runner accepts the baton

Upsweep method of handing baton

with the proper hand. Normally, the lead runner carries the baton in her right hand and hands it to the second runner in her left hand while standing in the outside part of her lane. This way, her left hand is positioned in the center of the lane.

The receiving hand alternates during the rest of the race. For instance, the second runner places the baton in the third runner's right hand as she stands on the inside of the lane. The third runner then places the baton in the anchor's left hand. This way, the baton stays in the middle of the lane all the way around the track, allowing the athletes to run the shortest distance.

Downsweep

This method was introduced in the 1960s and quickly became the most popular one. It differs greatly from the upsweep. For instance, the receiving runner's arm is held higher, almost parallel to the track, and the palm is pointing up instead of down. The incoming runner places the baton in her hand in a downward motion. This, too, is a blind pass.

The downsweep has several advantages. One, the receiving runner's arm is held higher and further from her body, reducing the chances of a collision with the incoming runner. Two, the runner with the baton has a better view of the receiver's hand. Three, the upward angle of the hand lessens the chance of a dropped baton.

Despite its popularity, the downsweep has disadvantages. For instance, the outgoing runner may not keep her arm high enough and straight enough to provide a good target for her teammate. In addition, the approaching runner often tends to raise the baton too high before passing it. This costs time and can disrupt rhythm. Finally, the incoming runner may extend her arm too soon, before she reaches her teammates. It's hard to run fast if your arms is "frozen" in front of you.

Downsweep method of handing baton (left and following page)

In each relay distance, the incoming runner should NEVER let go of the baton until she knows her teammate has it. She should feel the other athlete pull the baton from her hands. Don't simply place it in her hand, or the baton could easily fall to the track as she takes off.

The approaching runner should resist the temptation to slow down as she nears the other runner. Slowing down doesn't increase the chances of a smooth exchange—instead, it can disrupt rhythm while costing time. You want the baton to travel as fast as possible all the way around the track.

4 × 400 Meters

Unlike the 4 × 100, athletes in the 4 × 400 usually don't use a blind pass. Instead, the receiving runner turns to look at the runner with the baton. Here's the reason. The incoming runner is usually so tired, having sprinted an entire lap, that her strides have become uneven. It's hard to make a smooth handoff if you're weaving from side to side. In the 400 especially, the outgoing runner must grab the baton from the approaching runner to ensure a safe exchange. She needs to watch her teammate's strides as she approaches and get in the proper spot for a good handoff.

In both the 4 × 100 and 4 × 400, the baton should be exchange near the end of the 20-meter passing zone.

RESPONSIBILITIES OF EACH RUNNER IN THE 4 × 100 RELAY

Lead Runner

She must have strong acceleration out of the starting blocks. She cannot take off slowly and put her team in a hole. In addition, she must able to run well on curves without slowing down. She has to hug the inside of the curve to maintain top speed. Being the lead runner, she only has to worry about handing off the baton, not receiving it. But she must excel at handing it off. As you can imagine, it's demoralizing for a team to suffer a dropped baton during the first exchange.

Second Runner

This athlete runs the backstretch, a section that's almost a complete straightaway. Therefore, she can be a blazing sprinter without worrying about mastering curves. Unlike the lead runner, she has to pass and receive the baton. Some coaches have their fastest girl run second, hoping to pick up a big lead during the backstretch.

Third Runner

This athlete must be an excellent on curves because that's where most of her running occurs. It's her job to fly out of the final turn and put the anchor in a position to win the race. Obviously, she has to be outstanding at handing off the baton. All eyes will be on her as she makes the final handoff of the relay. She does not want to blow it.

Fourth Runner

The anchor has the most pressure, particularly in a close race. The fate of the whole team is resting on her shoulders as she takes the baton. Normally, a coach wants his fastest runner to be the anchor. She must also perform well when the stakes are high. She doesn't have to deal with curves or handing off the baton. Her job is simple: either maintain her team's lead or capture the lead while sprinting straight ahead. She must be a fierce competitor who can reach down. She must be able to summon a burst of speed when it counts.

RESPONSIBILITIES OF EACH RUNNER IN THE 4 × 400 RELAY

Lead Runner

She needs to put her team in the lead. Because this event requires more endurance than the 4 × 100 (each athletes runs four times as far), the lead runner has to have a good sense of pace. She can't fly out of the blocks and then get exhausted and stagger to the next runner. If she does, her teammates will have to frantically make up for her mistake. The lead runner, then, needs to be one of the fastest on the team.

Second Runner

She must keep the team in contention. Unlike the lead runner, she is allowed to come out of her lane and break for the inside of the track on the backstretch. She should expect and be able to handle jostling from opponents as they fight for position. She has to establish her spot on the track, then be comfortable running in traffic. Even if she's well behind when she takes the baton, she can't quit. The race can still be won in the third and fourth legs if she keeps the team close. After all, the team with a big lead may suddenly drop the baton. You never know.

Third Runner

When she takes the baton, the race gets even more interesting—the last half has begun. If she's in front when she starts out, she should extend the lead. If she's behind, she should close the gap as much as possible before handing off to the anchor.

Fourth Runner

The anchor in the 4 × 400 has the same pressure as the anchor in the 4 × 100. However, because the race is much longer she may have a larger lead when she takes the baton. Still, she should never get overconfident and coast. Many relays have been lost when the anchor takes it easy, instead of running her hardest and closing out the win.

RECORDS

(USA Track & Field does not keep youth records for the 4 × 200 relay.)

4 × 100 Meter Relay

WORLD RECORD

- 41.37 (East Germany—10/6/85)

U.S. NATIONAL RECORDS

- [ages 13–14]—46.89 (Essence Kendrick, Noel Dula, Shakerrah Merritt, Kamia Saulsberry of Long Beach, California, 7/28/96)
- [ages 15–16]—45.57 (A. Emanuel, B. Washington, C. Ratliff, M. Hall of Houston, Texas, 7/28/96)
- [ages 17–18]—45.02 (R. Caruthers, M. Edmonson, M. Withers, E. Grayson of Inglewood, California, 7/27/97)

4 × 400 Meter Relay

WORLD RECORD

- 3:15.17 (Soviet Union—10/1/88)

U.S. NATIONAL RECORDS

- [ages 13–14]—3:45.9 (Myleik Teele, Regine Caruthers, Malika Edmonson, Roshanna Payne of Inglewood, California, 7/29/93)
- [ages 15–16]—3:38.37 (Christina Smith, Tiffany Abney, Tiffany Bradley, Evelyn Dwyer of Philadelphia, Pennsylvania, 7/30/00)
- [ages 17–18]—3:39.49 (Evelyn Dwyer, Dominique Darden, Danielle Rogers, Tiffany Abney of Philadelphia, Pennsylvania, 7/29/01)

4 × 800 Meter Relay

WORLD RECORD

- 7:50.17 (Soviet Union—8/5/84)

U.S. NATIONAL RECORDS

- [ages 13–14]—9:17.51 (Keyotta Delemen, Shalonda Solomon, Treani Swain, Shante McKinney of Los Angeles, California, 7/28/99)
- [ages 15–16]—9:09.65 (Rachel Giannascoli, Evelyn Dwyer, Tiffany Abney, Alycia Williams of Philadelphia, Pennsylvania, 7/29/00)
- [ages 17–18]—8:53.93 (Danielle Rogers, Tiffany Abney, Jessica Davis, Evelyn Dwyer of Philadelphia, Pennsylvania, 7/28/01)

Source: USA Track & Field

FAULTS AND FIXES

Fault: The outgoing runner starts too soon or too late.
Result: Disrupts exchange, costs time.
Fix: More practice. Work on handoff over and over. Make sure the baton receiver knows where to be in relation to the incoming runner.

Fault: The receiver looks back during the exchange (in the 4 × 100).
Result: Throws off rhythm and speed of incoming runner.
Fix: Build more confidence in receiver. The blind pass requires excellent timing that can only come from repetition.

Fault: The two runners continually drop the baton during the exchange.
Result: Demoralizing for team, drastically reduces chances of victory.
Fix: Improve focus. Realize the importance of a smooth handoff. Coach should consider switching the runners. Maybe these two girls don't work well together. Perhaps there's a height difference that makes the exchange difficult. A coach may decide that a girl shouldn't be on the team.

Fault: The baton carrier extends her arm too soon toward the receiver.
Result: Disrupts her rhythm as she approaches. It's impossible to run your fastest with your arm sticking out for a long time.
Fix: Work on mechanics of the handoff. Learn the proper place to be on the track to reach out. Talk with baton receiver—maybe she hasn't mastered handoffs, and the incoming runner is trying to compensate.

Fault: The baton carrier slows down before the exchange.
Result: Costs time. Hurts the chances of a smooth handoff. Indicates she isn't confident in making a clean exchange.
Fix: Practice. Two runners should work together over and over. Maybe they aren't a good match and the coach should put them in a different position.

Fault: The incoming runner continually runs into the receiver.
Result: Disrupts rhythm, costs time. Can make receiver drop the baton or trip.
Fix: Study the boundaries of the passing zone. Learn where it starts and where it ends and the best place to make the exchange. Place a mark on the track where that should be, and run to it over and over.

Fault: Baton exchange occurs outside passing zone.
Result: Disqualification.
Fix: See above.

Fault: The incoming runner has difficulty placing the baton firmly in her teammate's hand.

Result: Both runners lose confidence, which may cause them to tense up.

Fix: The outgoing runner may have her hand incorrectly positioned. It should be open, with the thumb and forefinger forming a V. Otherwise, she's not providing a good target. Also, her arm should be at the proper height (almost parallel to track) and not waving back and forth.

She said it . . .

"My mother taught me very early to believe I could achieve any accomplishment I wanted to. The first was to walk without braces."

—Wilma Rudolph, who was diagnosed with polio when she was four but won a bronze medal in the 4 × 100 relay in the 1956 Olympics (at age 16) and a gold medal in the 4 × 100 in the 1960 Olympics.

DRILLS

Bottle Drill

Place an empty two-liter soda bottle on a table or stool (about 30 inches high). Stand three feet in front. Reach back as if you're receiving a baton. Pump your arms three or four times, then grab the bottle in a fluid, firm motion. Repeat.

Bounce Drill

Stand three feet in front of a wall. Hold a two-liter bottle in one hand (the one that receives the baton). Reach back almost to the wall and gently bounce the bottle off the wall and back into your hand several times. Creates a feel for receiving the baton.

Standing Handoffs

Four athletes stand in a straight line, 1.5 meters apart. The runner in back holds a baton, then passes it to the runner in front, who passes it in front of her, etc. When the athlete in front gets the baton, everyone turns around, and the drill is repeated. The athletes aren't running, so all their attention can be focused on learning to pass and receive the baton smoothly.

Jogging Handoffs

Four athletes stand on a track 50 meters apart. The runner in back starts with the baton and jogs toward the next athlete, then makes the exchange. The receiving runner does the same, passing the baton to the third runner, who passes it to the fourth. Then everyone turns around, and the drill is repeated. Try this variation: The incoming runner places the baton in her teammate's palm three times, pulling it

Practicing handoff while jogging (top and bottom photos)

back quickly each time, before releasing it. This repetition can increase confidence in the passer and receiver.

Acceleration Drill

Four athletes stand 100 meters apart on a track. The runner in back has the baton. She jogs 50 meters toward the next runner, then sprints the final 50 meters and makes the handoff. The next runner does the same, and so on, until the runner in front has the baton. This drill gives athletes the feel of running hard through the exchange.

Hit the Spot

Use chalk to mark a 20-meter passing zone at four spots on the track spaced 100 meters apart. Then make a mark five meters in front of each zone. Runners stand in the four zones. As the incoming runner steps on the mark five meters in front, the outgoing runner begins running and then takes the baton. This drill teaches the baton carrier and the receiver to be aware of their location on the track.

SUPERSTARS: THE RECORD-SETTING AMERICAN 4 × 100 RELAY TEAM

You've heard the phrase *Dream Team.* That certainly applies to the American relay team of Marion Jones, Gail Devers, Inger Miller, and Chryste Gaines. They set the American 4 × 100 relay record of 41.47 in 1997.

We've already talked about Marion and Gail. In the 2000 Olympics, you'll recall, Marion won three gold medals (100 meters, 200 meters, and 4 × 400 relay) and two bronze medals (long jump and 4 × 100). She's the first female track athlete to win five medals in one Olympics. Gail won the gold medal in the 100 meters in the 1992 and 1996 Olympics.

The other two members of the Dream Team were outstanding athletes too. Inger won a gold medal in the 1996 Olympics in the 4 × 100 team, running in the third position. That's the same position she ran on record-setting team in 1997. (Chryste Gaines ran first, Marion second and Gail fourth.) Inger also won the World Championships in the 200 meters in 1999.

She is the daughter of Lennox Miller, an Olympic medal winner in the 100 meters in 1968 and 1972. Inger began running during her sophomore year in high school and had immediate success. She clocked a 11.64 in the 100 meters (only 0.3 seconds

(continued)

(continued)

off the current 15- and 16-year-old record) and 23.59 in the 200 meters (only 0.33 seconds off the current record in that age group).

She says her father inspired her.

"Whatever he put his mind to, nothing could stop him," Inger said. "I'm just like that. I'm hardheaded and stubborn. When I make a decision about something, I stick to it."

During college, Inger excelled in track while doing well in class too. She graduated in 1994 from the University of Southern California with a degree in biological sciences/preveterinary medicine.

"My advice is this: Whatever it is you like to do—music, athletics, school, painting—your success comes down to self-discipline and willpower," she said. "If you want to do it, pursue it. Don't let anybody tell you *you can't.*"

Chryste is another top athlete who realizes the importance of academics. Her athletic record is impressive. She won a gold medal in the 4 × 100 relay in the 1996 Olympics and a bronze medal in same event in 2000. In addition, Chryste was the national 100 meter champion in 2001. But she also did well in the classroom. In 1994, Chryste graduated from Stanford University—one of the country's top academic schools—with a degree in psychology, while also completing her pre-med requirement. Chryste began running when she was 12, but her parents—a teacher and a lawyer—helped her to keep athletics in perspective.

"Homework first," Chryste remembers them saying.

Before the 2000 Olympics, she helped sponsor a nationwide writing contest for 13- and 14-year-olds. The top four boys and girls won a trip to the Olympics.

The topic for the paper: What does it take to become an Olympian.

That's a question any member of the Dream Team can answer.

SAMPLE WORKOUTS

4 × 100 METER RELAY (OFF-SEASON)	
Monday	Warm-up
	Stretching
	Sprint drills

	Five runs of 400–480 meters with six-minutes' rest at 50–60 percent of maximum Cooldown
Tuesday	Warm-up Stretching Sprint drills Eight 110-meter runs on a curve at 70–80 percent of maximum Weights
Wednesday	Warm-up Stretching Sprint drills Five runs of 300–400 meters with six-minutes' rest at 60–70 percent of maximum Cooldown
Thursday	Warm-up Stretching Sprint drills Plyometrics and standing long jumps Cooldown Weights
Friday	Warm-up Stretching Sprint drills Five runs of 300–400 meters with six-minutes' rest at 60–70 percent of maximum Cooldown
Saturday/Sunday	Rest

4 × 100 METER RELAY (EARLY SEASON)

Monday	Warm-up Stretching Sprint drills Five runs of 300–400 meters with six-minutes' rest at 70–80 percent of maximum Cooldown
Tuesday	Warm-up Stretching Sprint drills Eight 110-meter runs on curve at 70–80 percent maximum Relay handoffs Weights
Wednesday	Warm-up Stretching Sprint drills

4 × 100 METER RELAY (EARLY SEASON) *(continued)*	
	Five runs of 200–300 meters with six-minutes' rest at 75–90 percent of maximum Cooldown
Thursday	Warm-up Stretching Sprint drills Relay handoffs Cooldown Weights
Friday	Warm-up Stretching Sprint drills Five runs of 300–400 meters with six-minutes' rest at 70–80 percent of maximum Cooldown
Saturday/Sunday	Rest

4 × 100 METER RELAY (MID-SEASON)	
Monday	Warm-up Stretching Sprint drills Five runs of 160–200 meters with six-minutes' rest at 85–100 percent of maximum Cooldown
Tuesday	Warm-up Stretching Sprint drills Starts Relay handoffs Cooldown Weights
Wednesday	Warm-up Stretching Sprint drills Five runs of 120–200 meters with six-minutes' rest at 85–100 percent of maximum Cooldown
Thursday	Warm-up Stretching Sprint drills Starts Relay handoffs Cooldown Weights (upper body)

Friday	Competition or stretch and jog
Saturday	Competition or stretch and jog
Sunday	Rest

4 × 400 METER RELAY (OFF-SEASON)

Monday	Warm-up Stretching Sprint drills Five runs of 400–600 meters with six-minutes' rest at 50–70 percent of maximum Cooldown
Tuesday	Warm-up Stretching Sprint drills and plyometrics Eight 110-meter runs on a curve at 70–80 percent of maximum Weights
Wednesday	Warm-up Stretching Sprint drills Five runs of 400–600 meters with six-minutes' rest at 50–70 percent of maximum Cooldown
Thursday	Warm-up Stretching Sprint drills and plyometrics Eight 110-meter runs on a curve at 70–80 percent of maximum Weights
Friday	Warm-up Stretching Sprint drills Five runs of 400–600 meters with six-minutes' rest at 50–70 percent of maximum Cooldown
Saturday/Sunday	Rest

4 × 400 METER RELAY (EARLY SEASON)

Monday	Warm-up Stretching Sprint drills Five runs of 300–500 meters with six-minutes' rest at 65–85 percent of maximum Cooldown

4 × 400 METER RELAY (EARLY SEASON) *(continued)*	
Tuesday	Warm-up Stretching Sprint drills Practice 4 × 400 relay exchanges Eight 110-meter runs on a curve at 70–80 percent of maximum Weights
Wednesday	Warm-up Stretching Sprint drills Five runs of 300–500 meters with six-minutes' rest at 65–85 percent of maximum Cooldown
Thursday	Warm-up Stretching Sprint drills Practice 4 × 400 relay exchanges Eight 110-meter runs on a curve at 70–80 percent of maximum Weights
Friday	Warm-up Stretching Sprint drills Five runs of 300–500 meters with six-minutes' rest at 65–85 percent of maximum Cooldown
Saturday/Sunday	Rest

4 × 400 METER RELAY (MID-SEASON)	
Monday	Warm-up Stretching Sprint drills Two to four runs of 300–400 meters with eight-minutes' rest at 85–100 percent of maximum Cooldown
Tuesday	Warm-up Stretching Sprint drills Practice 4 × 400 relay exchanges Five 110-meter runs on a curve at 90–95 percent of maximum Weights
Wednesday	Warm-up Stretching

	Sprint drills Two to four runs of 300–400 meters with eight- minutes' rest at 85–100 percent of maximum Cooldown
Thursday	Warm-up Stretching Sprint drills Practice 4 × 400 relay exchanges Five 110-meter runs on a curve at 90–95 percent of maximum Weights
Friday	Competition or stretch and jog
Saturday	Competition or stretch and jog
Sunday	Rest

She said it . . .
"You have to believe in yourself. The ones who believe in themselves the most are the ones who win."

—Florence Griffith-Joyner, gold medal winner
in 4 × 100 relay in 1988 Olympics.

6
JUMPING EVENTS

The jumping events, when done properly, are beautiful and graceful. The high jump, long jump, triple jump, and pole vault are individual events that have some similarities. In each, athletes must temporarily overcome gravity to jump high or long. Top jumpers almost appear to be flying, suspended off the earth's surface as they strive for another fraction of an inch.

The long jump and triple jump are the most similar of the jumping events. Both require a speedy approach and powerful horizontal leap into a pit of sand. In the high jump and pole vault, athletes clear the bar in dramatically different manners. For instance, in the high jump, competitors go over the bar head first, with their back facing the ground. In the pole vault, athletes clear the bar feet first, aided by a flexible pole that catapults them to great heights.

The pole vault is almost in a category by itself. Competitors use their arms and shoulders much more than in other jumping events. The training and conditioning, therefore, are different. The pole vault is the newest event open to women. It became a women's Olympic event in 2000.

Pole vaulting launches athletes to great heights and can be one of the most exciting jumping events. The current national record for teens is more than 12 feet, $7^1/4$ inches. Naturally, leaping that high might scare some people, for good reason. Pole vaulting can be dangerous. Unfortunately, competitors are occasionally seriously injured or even killed when they fail to land on the mat. For that reason, safety is an issue in the pole vault. Recently, the thick mats in the landing pit have been made even larger to increase the chances of a safe landing.

With proper training and precautions, pole vaulting can be safe and enjoyable. Because it's a new event for women, they can feel like pioneers in the sport.

This chapter begins with a discussion of the high jump, followed by a discussion of the long jump, triple jump, and pole vault. Each event has unique techniques that involve the whole body. In the jumping events, especially, don't start before you understand the basics. Otherwise, you can get hurt or develop bad habits that will hurt your performance.

HIGH JUMP

Today's high jumpers clear heights that would have been unimaginable a few decades ago. Much of the improvement has come from better training and improvement in high-jumping technique.

The event was revolutionized in 1968 by a jumper from Oregon named Dick Fosbury. In the Olympics that year, he stunned fellow competitors by going over the bar backwards, an entirely new concept. Until then, high jumpers used the straddle method, clearing the bar with their bodies horizontal and face down.

Fosbury won a gold medal and also set a world record in the 1968 Olympics. Other high jumpers quickly adopted his technique, which came to be known as the Fosbury Flop. Today, virtually all competitors use it because it's relatively easy to learn and very effective.

In the high jump, it helps to have natural jumping ability. But high jumpers who consistently excel must master complex mechanics that aren't visible to the casual spectator. We've said it before, but it's worth saying again: Hard work and dedication can win out over talent alone.

Sometimes, coaches recruit high jumpers from the basketball and volleyball teams. Those sports also require tremendous jumping ability and body control. When athletes dunk a basketball or spike a volleyball, they are using some of the same movements as high jumpers. A good test for athletes considering the high jump is the vertical jump. It's very simple. You stand against a gym wall and jump as high as you can from a standing position. A coach marks the highest spot you reach. This is a good measure of natural jumping ability but it's no guarantee of success in the high jump.

High jumping also requires a fast run-up to the bar and an ability to arch your body backward while also rotating sideways. High jumpers must spend hours on their technique to learn the correct position for their feet, legs, hips, arms, shoulders, and head. These complex mechanics must become second nature. If you stop to think of any of them during competition, you won't be able to achieve the fluid motion that's required.

The high jump can be an exhilarating event. It's fun to jump higher and higher, then fall back on the mats and see the bar still in place. You feel like you've defied gravity for a moment.

The high jump is taught in three main parts: the approach, the takeoff, and bar clearance. All must be mastered to achieve success. We will discuss them in detail later in the chapter.

THE BASICS

- The high jump was one of the original events in the first modern Olympics in Athens in 1896 (for men). It became a women's Olympic event in 1928.
- Competitors are disqualified after three straight failures. If the crossbar falls off after they have landed on the cushion, it's still a failed jump.
- The crossbar is raised two centimeters at a time as athletes clear a height.
- The bar is circular and made of fiberglass. It cannot be more than three centimeters in diameter or weigh more than two kilograms (four pounds, 6.5 ounces). The bar may sag up to two centimeters in the middle.
- The jump must be made off one foot only.
- The run-up area before the crossbar must be at least 15 millimeters long. Competitors may start as far back as they like.
- Athletes are allowed to use markers to guide their run-up and takeoff.
- The cushioned landing area is five meters wide and three meters deep.
- Competitors may pass at any height and wait for the bar to be raised before attempting their jump.
- Athletes are allowed a minute and a half to complete each jump.
- The shoe on the athlete's jumping foot has cleats under the front and back. The sole must be no more than 13 millimeters thick. Competitors may wear a normal athletic shoe on the other foot.

TECHNIQUE

Approach

The approach is the foundation of the high jump. If you don't generate enough speed and momentum, you won't be able to clear a respectable height. In that sense, the most important part of the jump occurs before you leave the ground. Because of this, 90 percent of your training should focus on the approach.

Once you're in the air, there's little you can do to make your body go higher. Your height is primarily determined by your technique as you approach. For example, you would never think of standing in front of the bar and trying to jump over it flat-footed. You need a strong approach run to generate height.

Each high jumper must determine the proper number of steps for their run-up. This is extremely important. During a meet, you never want to

Lining up for approach run

Approach run toward bar (above and following page)

guess at how many steps to take as you approach the bar. With the help of your coach, you should try different approach lengths until you find the number of steps that work best for you.

Most high jumpers take about 10 steps. Once you determine the best number for you, stick with it and practice your approach over and over. Repetition is absolutely critical. You must learn to be consistent. Think of it as choreographing your launch.

This might sound a bit mechanical. You might think you can simply rely on your jumping ability and do what feels comfortable that day. Wrong. In the pressure of a meet, it's easy to get rattled. If your approach hasn't become second-nature, you're likely to be tentative as you approach the bar. Remember, repetition in practice produces rhythm during competition.

An important part of the high jump is determining your jumping foot. Everyone is more comfortable jumping off one foot than the other. Earlier in the book, we discussed identifying your lead foot for sprinting—the one you place in the back of the starting blocks. The proper takeoff foot is as important in the high jump as the lead foot is in sprints. Experiment until you determine your takeoff foot.

Once you do, it's time to work on the approach. If you're jumping off your left foot, start about 10 to 15 feet right of the supports for the crossbar. If you're jumping off your right foot, start the same distance to the left.

To start, place your takeoff foot in front and make a firm step forward with your other foot. Your approach should look like a J. You start running straight and then, about four steps later, gradually begin curving toward the middle of the bar.

When you're making the curve, lean your whole body slightly away from the bar. This helps you get into a stronger jumping position. Your next-to-last step should be your longest. A long step lowers your body's center of gravity and loads your thighs with power to make a high jump.

Your final step should be just to the right of the center of the bar (for people jumping off their left foot). As you jump and arch backward, your momentum will naturally carry you sideways to the left. That's okay. Don't fight it. Just be sure to start your jump to the right of the bar's center so you won't go so far to the left that you miss the mats. That hurts, and it's dangerous.

Be sure to make smooth strides and gradually increase your speed as you approach the bar. Don't start too fast or you will decelerate in your final steps and make a weak jump. As you practice, you will begin to feel the proper speed and rhythm.

Takeoff

On your final step, your plant foot should be angled and pointing inside the far standard, the support piece holding up the crossbar. As you jump, think of rotating *around* the bar, not going straight over it. Determine your exact spot to take off then practice reaching that spot over and over.

As you jump, your weight should be directly over your plant foot, and your body should be erect. Push upward with your toes as you jump. Pull your arms as far back behind your shoulders as you can and keep them close to your sides. Then thrust them forward to help you get higher. At the same time, bend and raise your non-jumping leg.

Start of jump

Clearing the bar with back arched

Landing on shoulder and upper back

Finally, tilt your head back and raise your chin. This, too, helps you reach a greater height.

Clearing the Bar

When you reach the bar, your head and back should pass over first. Be sure to arch your back and look up to avoid hitting the bar. Once your upper body has cleared, pull your feet to your buttocks and arms to your sides. This makes it easier for your lower body to rotate over the bar. As your hips clear, drop your chin to your chest and straighten your knees so that your feet don't knock off the bar.

Once your whole body is over the bar, it's important to land properly. You want to come down on your upper back and shoulder, not on your neck. That can produce serious injury, even with thickly cushioned mats. Over time, you should develop a consistent landing position, the same way you develop a consistent approach and jump.

RECORDS

WORLD RECORD

- 6'10.25" (Stefka Kostadinova—Bulgaria, 8/30/87)

U.S. NATIONAL RECORDS

- [ages 13–14]—5'8.5" (Chrissy Mills of Tarzana, California, 6/8/86)
- [ages 15–16]—5'11" (Camee Williams of Dayton, Ohio, 7/28/96)
- [ages 17–18]—6'1" (Adrianne Sims of Fayetteville, North Carolina, 7/24/97)

Source: USA Track & Field

FAULTS AND FIXES

Fault: Athlete is tentative as she approaches the bar.
Result: Slows down, loses momentum necessary for a good jump.
Fix: Practice steps over and over, until you can make the same steps every time. This breeds confidence and produces better jumps.

Fault: Plants lead foot too far from bar.
Result: Achieves adequate height but loses momentum and comes down on top of the bar.
Fix: Work on approach steps with your coach. Find the exact spot to jump. It's a little different for everyone. Mark that spot and practice hitting it with your lead foot over and over, without jumping. Once your approaches are consistent, you can begin to jump.

Fault: Takeoff foot is too close to bar.
Result: You hit bar with upper body as you jump.
Fix: Plant takeoff foot further from the bar. This gives you the room to make a higher vertical jump and clear the bar. Once you've found your best takeoff spot, practice running to it.

Fault: Takeoff position is okay, but athlete leans into the bar while jumping, instead of staying vertical.
Result: Hit bar.
Fix: Lengthen the last two approach steps. This creates speed and momentum and allows you to make an explosive vertical jump over the bar, instead of a weak jump into the bar.

Fault: Athlete takes off with back turned completely to the bar, instead of angled in.
Result: Weak takeoff, limited height.

Fix: Work on approach, especially the last step and takeoff. Sometimes athletes instinctively turn their backs to the bar because they haven't mastered the tempo of the approach. You want to jump, then turn your back completely, to get the proper rotation and maximum height.

Fault: Steps and takeoff position are fine, but athlete can't seem to jump high enough.
Result: Consistently fails to clear bar.
Fix: Analyze several elements of your technique. Problem could be: (1) failing to create a firm base by having your weight over your takeoff foot, (2) failing to draw your arms back and thrust them forward for added height, (3) failing to raise your chin off your chest as you rise.

Fault: Athlete achieves adequate height and clears with upper body, but the legs consistently hit bar.
Result: Destroys confidence, can undermine other elements of the jump.
Fix: Work on arching your back, pulling your feet against your buttocks and bringing your arms to your side. These movements increase body rotation. Once your hips clear, dip your chin toward your chest. This helps pull your thighs over the bar. Finally, straighten your knees to let your feet clear.

DRILLS

One-Legged Hurdle Hops

Place five low hurdles on a track in a straight line, about four meters apart. Hop with your takeoff leg only, clearing each hurdle, landing and then immediately hopping over the next one. Hold your non-takeoff leg for stability. Builds power and explosiveness necessary for high jumping.

Single-Leg Dips

Stand upright on your takeoff leg with your arms at your side. Slowly bend your knee and

One-legged hurdle hops

Single-leg dips

lower your body 45 degrees. Keep your heel on the ground. Then straighten your knee and raise your body to an upright position. This creates strong thigh muscles, necessary for good vertical lift.

Beginning Jumping

This drill gives new high jumpers the feel of jumping with their back to the bar and landing on the mats. No bar is used. Stand about three feet in front of the landing pit, with your heels facing the mats. Jump as high as you can, lifting your hips and arms, then raising your legs as you fall back onto the mats. Repeat twice.

Figure Eights

Using cones, set up a figure eight course about 20 meters long. Run close to full speed, leaning toward the center of the eight. To do so, you will alternate leaning with your right shoulder, then left shoulder. This leaning motion simulates the posture your body needs to be in as you approach the bar and prepare to jump. Run the course four times.

High-Stepping

Run 50 meters in a straight line on a track or field. Consciously raise your knees toward your chest until they are parallel to the ground. This produces the feel to elevating your knees as you jump and then clear the bar. Run the distance four times.

Bounding

Begin jogging and take long, skipping strides, landing and pushing off with one foot, then the other. As you do, swing your arms together forward and backward. The bounding strides are similar to your approach steps, and the arm motion teaches you to swing your arms upward as you jump for added height.

Figure eights

Approach Practice

Mark your steps in a J pattern from the start of your approach to take-off. At first, walk your approach. Learn to feel where your steps should be. Once you become comfortable, job the approach a few times. Then run at regular speed, accelerating as you prepare to jump. Repeat three times without jumping.

SAMPLE WORKOUTS

	HIGH JUMP (OFF-SEASON)
Monday	Jog two laps as warm-up Stretch Sprint drills on grass Ten 60-meter buildup runs Weights
Tuesday	Jog two laps as warm-up Stretch

	Sprint drills on grass Circle runs (work on leaning inward) Single-leg hops Bench hops Hurdle hops
Wednesday	Jog two laps as warm up Stretch Sprint drills on grass Ten 60-meter buildup runs Weights
Thursday	Jog two laps Stretch Sprint drills on grass Circle runs (work on leaning inward) Single-leg hops Bench hops Hurdle hops
Friday	Jog two laps Stretch Sprint drills on grass Ten 60-meter buildup runs Weights
Saturday/Sunday	Rest

HIGH JUMP (EARLY SEASON)	
Monday	Jog two laps Stretch Sprint drills on grass Approach runs (work on steps) Practice jumping off platform Weights
Tuesday	Jog two laps Stretch Sprint drills on grass Approach runs (work on steps) Three-step jumps Full approach jumps
Wednesday	Jog two laps Stretch Sprint drills on grass Approach runs (work on steps) Jump off platform Weights
Thursday	Jog two laps Stretch

HIGH JUMP (EARLY SEASON) *(continued)*	
	Sprint drills on grass
	Approach runs (work on steps)
	Three-step jumps
Friday	Competition or rest
Saturday	Competition
Sunday	Rest

HIGH JUMP (MID-SEASON)	
Monday	Jog two laps
	Stretch
	Sprint drills on grass
	Approach runs (work on steps)
	Jump off platform
	Weights
Tuesday	Jog two laps
	Stretch
	Sprint drills on grass
	Approach runs
	Three-step jumps
	Full approach jumps
Wednesday	Jog two laps
	Stretch
	Sprint drills on grass
	Approach runs
	Jumping off platform
	Weights
Thursday	Jog two laps
	Stretch
	Sprint drills on grass
	Approach runs
	Three-step jumps
	Full approach jumps
Friday	Competition or rest
Saturday	Competition
Sunday	Rest

LONG JUMP

The long jump has many similarities to the high jump. Each requires a powerful, but measured, approach run with carefully rehearsed steps. Just as in the high jump, success in the long jump depends almost entirely on a proper run-up. Once you've left the ground, there's little you can do to extend your jump.

The watershed moment in the high jump occurred in 1968. That's when a relatively unknown American, Dick Fosbury, used his backward jumping style at the Olympics, set a world record, and took the gold medal.

At the same Olympics in Mexico City, another American, Bob Beamon, shattered previous notions of the long jump. He jumped an astounding 29'2". Beamon's record stood for more than 20 years.

Young athletes today keep jumping further and further. Many current junior records exceed those of storied Olympians in years past. For instance, the current U.S. teenage record in the long jump is 20 feet, 10$^1/2$ inches. That's a half-inch farther than the women's gold medal winner in the 1960 Olympics.

More records will surely be set. Perhaps your name will be in the sports record books someday. Learn the proper technique, and anything is possible.

THE BASICS

- Athletes jump into a sand pit at least nine meters long and 2.75 meters wide. The pit begins at least a meter beyond the takeoff line.
- The sand is moistened slightly before competition and is raked even with the runway after each jump.
- The runway must be at least 40 meters long. Just as in the high jump, athletes may start as far back as they like.
- Athletes make three or six jumps, depending on the number of competitors. They can take up to a minute and a half for each try. Competitors may place one or two markers along the runway to guide their steps.
- The takeoff board is made of wood and is 20 centimeters wide. It is level with the runway. Athletes may step on the board, but their plant foot can not extend beyond the edge closest to the pit. Beyond the takeoff board is a 10-centimeter band of a soft substance called Plasticine. The athletes' cleats leave a mark if she jumps beyond the takeoff mark. That represents a foul.
- Fouls also occur if a competitor tries to somersault in the air to gain distance, or if she lands and then steps backward in the pit.
- After each jump, a judge raises a white flag to indicate a successful jump or a red flag to signal a foul.
- Two judges mark the length of the jump. The distance is measured from the first impression in the sand back to the takeoff line.
- Long jump became a women's Olympic event in 1948.

TECHNIQUE

The long jump consists of three elements: approach, takeoff, and airborne action. We'll spend the most time on the approach because, as in all jumping events, it's the most critical.

Approach

The number of steps taken by long jumpers tends to vary more than those of high jumpers.

In the long jump, successful competitors may take 12 to 20 strides. For high school girls, 16 to 18 is the norm. In theory, more steps produce greater speed and a longer jump. But many young athletes find it hard to maintain a consistent stride if they take too many steps. They may also decelerate as they approach their jump. Deceleration is particularly bad. You must have a powerful approach to make a winning jump. So, you want speed but *controlled* speed.

Good conditioning helps athletes maintain rhythm with a long run-up. Still, some athletes in outstanding shape jump further with fewer steps. Work with your coach and figure out the best number of steps for you. That number should allow you to reach your take-off spot without extending or shortening your steps. If you're fiddling with your steps as you approach takeoff, you're much more likely to run past the takeoff line and foul or jump too soon and not go very far.

A good approach depends on the first two or three strides. If your initial steps are out of sync, it's hard to gain the proper tempo and confidence to make a strong jump.

Just as in the high jump, mark your steps during practice and rehearse them repeatedly. Also, determine your takeoff foot early on. Everyone has a clear preference. Some athletes begin their approach with the same foot they use for jumping. Others begin with one foot and take off with the other. Find out what works best for you. In either case, begin your approach with a firm step forward to establish a fluid motion. Also, lean forward slightly at first, then gradually rise to an upright position.

For your final two steps, you should be running full speed. The next-to-last stride needs to be the longest because that will lower your body slightly and let you load more power into your jumping leg. Plant your foot flat on the runway and feel as if you're gathering yourself for the jump.

The last step is when you jump. If it's too long, your body will tend to brake. You'll lose the necessary explosiveness. In the last two steps, be sure to pump your arms to help generate power for the jump.

Takeoff

On the last step, your foot should be flat against the track and directly in front of your body. This allows you to make the highest vertical leap. By contrast, if you step on the front of your foot, your body won't be stable enough to make a powerful jump.

You should look ahead and slightly up, not down at the takeoff board. That tends to make you tentative. You want to explode into the air with your body fully upright. After you jump, continue to move your legs as if you're still running. Imagine sprinting in the air.

Plant at takeoff

Airborne Action

As we've said, once you leave the ground you really can't increase the length of your jump. It's already been determined by the quality of your approach. However, proper airborne technique keeps your body from rotating forward too far and, as a result, puts you in a position to land cleanly.

While in the air, most long jumpers use the *hitch-kick* technique. This is the running motion we just described. Basically, you rotate your arms and legs forward in a circular motion. Without doing so, your forward motion can cause you to land head first in the sand.

Two other techniques some athletes use in the air are the

In the air, using hitch-kick method

In air, using hang method

Sail technique and landing in pit

hang and the *sail.* In the hang, the athlete's upper body is vertical, and she extends her arms straight upward and slightly behind her head. She pulls her lower legs up to a 90-degree angle. Her body then hangs in the air during the jump. To land, she snaps her legs forward and down to the sand.

The sail technique, by comparison, is the simplest to learn but can be the least effective. In it, the high jumper gets into the landing position immediately after take off—legs horizontal and pointing straight out. She then sails through the air until landing. However, it's difficult with this technique to keep the body stable throughout the jump. You're likely to rotate forward and land too soon, losing distance or coming down with your upper body leading the way.

In any of the three techniques, you need to fully extend your arms forward and sweep them down as you prepare to land. This causes your legs to rise to a horizontal position too. For a brief moment, your arms and legs are parallel and close together.

Once your feet hit the sand, you should bend your knees to soften the impact and bring your arms forward to avoid falling back.

RECORDS

WORLD RECORD

- 24'8.25"—(Galina Chistyakova—Soviet Union, 6/11/88)

U.S. NATIONAL RECORDS

- [ages 13–14]—19'11" (Tracee Thomas of Rialto, California, 6/20/98)
- [ages 15–16]—20'2.5" (Jill Bell of Bellevue, Washington, 7/10/99)
- [ages 17–18]—20'10.5" (Angela Henry of Omaha, Nebraska, 7/29/94)

Source: USA Track & Field

FAULTS AND FIXES

Fault: Athlete consistently fouls.
Result: Loses confidence, technique breaks down.
Fix: Work on approach. Determine correct number of steps, jumping foot, takeoff spot. Rehearse run-ups without jumping. Repeated fouls can be traced to faulty approaches.

Fault: Decelerating or taking uneven strides as athlete approaches takeoff.
Result: Weak jump, poor distance.
Fix: Try reducing the number of approach steps. The more steps you take, the greater the chances of decelerating or getting out of sync. Improved conditioning can help. However, even some top jumpers prefer taking fewer steps. Experiment.

Fault: Approach, takeoff are okay, but jumps are too short.
Result: Breakdown in confidence, can undermine rhythm on upcoming jumps.
Fix: Look at several possibilities: (1) Your next-to-last step might be too short, preventing adequate lowering of the body and loading of legs. (2) Your final step could be on the front of your foot, instead of flat-footed. This keeps you from establishing a stable base for maximum height. (3) You aren't pumping your arms enough. Proper arm movement creates speed and lift. (4) You're focusing your eyes down at takeoff, instead of straight and up slightly. Looking down makes it harder to jump high and long.

Fault: Body rotates forward while airborne.
Result: Legs don't achieve proper extension, distance suffers. Worse, you can make a painful landing on your head or shoulders.
Fix: Work on airborne technique. Try the hitch-kick method, the most common method of airborne action. In it, you rotate your arms and legs forward in a circle as if you're still running. Most athletes and coaches believe this is the best method to keep your body in an upright position and ready to land.

DRILLS

Run-Ups

Mark approach steps. Walk from starting position to jumping position. Become familiar with each step. Don't jump—concentrate only on steps. After walking approach steps twice, jog them twice, then run them are regular speed twice.

Lunges

From a standing start, step forward as far as you can with right leg. Let your left knee bend and touch the ground. Keep your right heel on the ground. Feel your body sink and extend forward. Hold for 10 seconds. Repeat, stepping forward with left leg.

Single-Leg Hops

Stand and grab your left ankle and pull it toward your buttocks. Now hop on your right leg for 30 meters. Rest briefly, then jump on your left leg while holding your right leg. Repeat once with each leg.

Standing Long Jump

Stand on the takeoff board. Pull your arms back and leap as far as you can up and out. As you land, bring your arms and legs together simultaneously. Repeat.

Lunging

Jumping Rope

Jump rope in place for three minutes. Then jump rope while slowly jogging forward for 50 meters. Then jump rope while jogging backwards for 50 meters.

Step-Ups

Find a box that's about two feet tall. Stand on the left side, then step onto the box with your right leg. Now, bring your left leg up. Step down on the other side with your right leg, then left. Repeat, stepping up first with the left leg, followed by the right.

Standing long jump (above and right)

Step-ups on box (above and right)

SAMPLE WORKOUTS

	LONG JUMP (OFF-SEASON)
Monday	Jog two laps as a warm-up Stretch Sprint drills on grass Ten 60-meter buildup runs Weights
Tuesday	Jog two laps as a warm-up Stretch Sprint drills on grass Single-leg hops Lunges Bench hops Hurdle hops
Wednesday	Jog two laps Stretch Sprint drills on grass Ten 60-meter buildup runs Weights
Thursday	Jog two laps Stretch Sprint drills on grass Single-leg hops Lunges Bench hops Hurdle hops
Friday	Jog two laps Stretch Sprint drills on grass Ten 60-meter buildup runs Weights
Saturday/Sunday	Rest

	LONG JUMP (EARLY SEASON)
Monday	Jog two laps Stretch Sprint drills on grass Standing long jumps into pit Approach runs on track Four-step jumps Weights

LONG JUMP (EARLY SEASON) *(continued)*	
Tuesday	Jog two laps Stretch Sprint drills on grass Approach runs on track Four-step jumps Full approach jumps
Wednesday	Jog two laps Stretch Sprint drills on grass Standing long jumps into pit Approach runs on track Four-step jumps Weights
Thursday	Jog two laps Stretch Sprint drills on grass Approach runs on track Four-step jumps Full approach jumps
Friday	Competition or rest
Saturday	Competition
Sunday	Rest

LONG JUMP (MID-SEASON)	
Monday	Jog two laps Stretch Sprint drills on grass Approach runs on track Four-step jumps Weights
Tuesday	Jog two laps Stretch Sprint drills on grass Approach runs on track Full approach runs
Wednesday	Jog two laps Stretch Sprint drills on grass Standing long jumps into pit Approach runs on track Weights
Thursday	Jog two laps Stretch

	Sprint drills on grass
	Standing long jumps into pit
	Approach runs on track
	Four-step jumps
Friday	Competition or rest
Saturday	Competition or rest
Sunday	Rest

TRIPLE JUMP

The triple jump is an unusual event that can be difficult to master. It consists of three different types of jumps that must be coordinated to produce the longest total distance. The event is demanding because it requires controlled speed, strength, balance, and timing. Unlike events like sprinting, the triple jump is not instinctive. It requires study and repeated practice. However, the rewards are great. There's satisfaction in teaching your body a complex series of moves that mesh in harmony. You also can be proud that you've learned an event that many won't even attempt.

THE BASICS

- The triple jump is one of the newest women's Olympic events, added in 1996.
- Competitors make three attempts during qualifying. Those with the best results advance to the finals and make three more attempts.
- The name of the event is a misnomer. Instead of making three jumps, athletes actually make a hop, a long step, then a jump.
- For the hop, athletes must land on the same foot they used for takeoff. For the step, they land on the opposite foot. For the jump, they land with both legs outstretched and together.
- Just as in the long jump, athletes can place two markers on the runway to guide their steps. In this event too, they must complete their jump within a minute and a half.
- A foul occurs if an athlete begins her hop beyond the takeoff mark or doesn't reach the landing pit during her jump.
- The length of the approach is unlimited. Most competitors make their run-up about 40 meters.
- Each of the three parts—the hop, step and jump—should be about the same length. The hop is usually the longest.

TECHNIQUE

To explain the triple jump, we'll describe each of the three phases: the hop, step, and jump. However, don't get the idea that they exist in isolation. Each phase builds on the previous one. The result should be a seamless flow from hop to step to jump, not an abrupt transition. To achieve this rhythm, you must understand the mechanics of each phase and practice them repeatedly.

Hop

To prepare for this first phase, you need a strong approach run, just as in the long jump. Beginners should make their approach about 30 meters. As you become better, you can extend it to gain more speed. However, if the approach becomes too long, you're likely to get out of sync or decelerate. Both lead to a weak hop. If this phase is weak, it's hard to win the event with a good step and jump.

The hop is different from the other phases because you take off and land on the same foot. In the step, by contrast, you leap on one foot and come down on the other.

Hop phase

For the hop, you should be running full speed—but still under control—when you reach the takeoff mark. If your arms and legs are flying wildly to help you go faster, you won't be able to get in a stable takeoff position.

Just as in the long jump, you should feel as if you're running off the board when you enter the air. Keep your body upright and concentrate on going out for greater distance, instead of up. Your arms must coordinate with your legs for best results.

Some athletes swing both arms forward simultaneously as they hop. This is called a double-arm technique. Others prefer a single-arm method, with one arm forward and the other behind. Experiment. The single-arm method seems more natural and rhythmic for most people. However, some athletes think using both arms gives them more strength for a longer hop.

The next-to-last step before you make the hop should be long. This lowers your body and loads power into your legs. This step and the final step should be flat-footed to provide a strong base.

Once you're airborne, remain vertical with your arms pulled back behind your chest and the knee of your lead leg bent. Try to glide through the air in this position.

To land, you should come down slightly on your heel, although mainly flat-footed. This lets you "roll" forward on your foot and move into the step phase. By contrast, if you land on your toes, you'll decelerate and lose rhythm.

Your hop should equal about 35 percent of the length of all three phases.

Step

The step is the most difficult phase. To prepare for it, pull your arms behind your torso. Most athletes like to bring the arms forward together as they step. This is the double-arm method we described above. At takeoff, your last step should be flat against the runway, with your eyes focused straight ahead. Your upper body leans forward slightly to maintain momentum, and your arms extend a bit from the side for balance.

As you go through the air, your landing leg is in front, bent at a 90-degree angle with the toes pointing up. Your other leg is behind your body with the heel raised near the buttocks. This posture is sometimes called a "moving statue" position.

To land, extend your lead leg and come down almost flat-footed, just slightly on your heel. Just as in the hop, this foot position gives you a stable base to land and move into the next phase.

Your step should be about 30 percent of the total distance.

Step phase

Jump

This jump phase in the long jump is similar to the long jump event. In both, you're leaping as far as you can horizontally into a sand pit. However, in the "jump" phase of the triple jump, you won't go as far. By the time you reach this last stage, you will have lost much of the momentum from your approach run.

The key is to squeeze as much length out of your jump as you can. To do this, most athletes use both arms (the double arm method) as they jump. This provides the best forward momentum. Unlike the previous stages, the jump should be *up*, as well as *out*. Your upper body needs to remain upright. Also, don't let your head lean backward. This tends to put the brakes on your jump.

When you're in the air, don't try to use the hitch-kick we described in the long jump: there's not enough time because your leap in the triple jump won't be as long. Instead, use the hang style. Remember, your arms should extend straight up and slightly behind your body. Your legs bend at a 90-degree angle. Your body becomes vertical, hanging in the air.

The landing is identical to the landing in the long jump. You should extend both arms horizontally in front and sweep them downward. This makes your legs rise to a horizontal position. Land on your heels, then bend your knees to lessen the impact and bring your arms forward to avoid falling back.

Jump

Landing in pit with sail technique

RECORDS

WORLD RECORD

- 50'10.25" (Inessa Kravets—Ukraine, 8/10/95)

U.S. NATIONAL RECORDS

- [ages 13–14]—39'1" (Nicole Duhart of Downey, California, 4/24/99)
- [ages 15–16]—41'1.25" (Deana Simons of Decatur, Illinois, 7/11/93)
- [ages 17–18]—42'8.25" (Alicia Broussard of Houston, Texas, 7/28/96)

Source: USA Track & Field

FAULTS AND FIXES

Fault: The first phase, the hop, is too short.
Result: Makes a good overall performance almost impossible.
Fix: Analyze approach. You may be taking too many steps. This can cause you to lose rhythm or decelerate as you approach takeoff.

Fault: You frequently make stutter steps as you near takeoff in all three phases.
Result: Dramatically shortens distance.
Fix: Practice steps over and over until they are automatic. During competition, you don't want to think about where to place your feet.

Fault: Steps seem fine, but distance remains short.
Result: Little chance of winning.
Fix: Consider the following: (1) Your final step before takeoff might be too long. This causes your body to overextend and brake. (2) The next-to-last stride might be too short. This prevents your body from lowering and your legs from loading for takeoff. (3) Your arm movement could be incorrect. Experiment with both the single- and double-arm methods—bringing forward one, or both arms, as you leave the ground.

Fault: At the end of your hop and step, you land on your toes or heels, instead of virtually flat-footed.
Result: Loss of momentum, distance.
Fix: Practice landing slightly on your heels, but mainly flat-footed. This gives you a stable base and lets you roll over your foot into the next phase. If you land on your toes, you'll decelerate and lose balance. If you land entirely on your heels, you fall backward and lose your momentum.

Bounding

DRILLS

Bounding

Take extremely long strides, landing on one foot briefly, then pushing off and landing on the other. Continue to alternate for 30 meters. Repeat. Be sure your body stays upright.

Box Stepping

Get five boxes or benches about 18 inches high and 12 inches wide. Space them three steps apart. Begin at one end and jog toward the first box. Step onto the box with your right leg, then down to the ground with your left. Continue this way until you've stepped on all the boxes.

Two-legged hurdle hops

Repeat, stepping onto the boxes with your left leg and down with your right. [*Note: be sure the boxes are strong enough to support your weight and stable enough not to slide as you step onto them.*]

Box Jumping

Using the same boxes, jump over the boxes, instead of onto them. Land on alternate feet and push off quickly. Clear all the boxes, then repeat.

Hurdle Hops

Place six low hurdles in a line on a track or a field. Stand at one end, bend your knees slightly and jump off both feet over the first hurdle. Bring both arms together simultaneously as you jump for extra power. Land on both feet, then hop over the remaining hurdles in the same way.

SAMPLE WORKOUTS

TRIPLE JUMP (OFF-SEASON)	
Monday	Jog two laps Stretch Sprint drills on grass Ten 60-meter buildup runs Weights
Tuesday	Jog two laps Stretch Sprint drills on grass Single-leg hops Lunges Bench hops Hurdle hops
Wednesday	Jog two laps Stretch Sprint drills on grass Ten 60-meter build-up runs Weights
Thursday	Jog two laps Stretch Sprint drills on grass Single-leg hops Lunges Bench hops Hurdle hops
Friday	Jog two laps Stretch Sprint drills on grass Ten 60-meter buildup runs Weights
Saturday/Sunday	Rest

TRIPLE JUMP (EARLY SEASON)	
Monday	Jog two laps Stretch Sprint drills on grass Standing triple jumps into pit Approach runs on track Weights
Tuesday	Jog two laps Stretch

	TRIPLE JUMP (EARLY SEASON) *(continued)*
	Sprint drills on grass
	Standing triple jumps into pit
	Approach runs on track
	Four-step jumps
Wednesday	Jog two laps
	Stretch
	Sprint drills on grass
	Standing triple jumps into pit
	Approach runs on track
	Weights
Thursday	Jog two laps
	Stretch
	Sprint drills on grass
	Standing triple jumps into pit
	Approach runs on track
	Four-step jumps
Friday	Competition or rest
Saturday	Competition
Sunday	Rest

	TRIPLE JUMP (MID-SEASON)
Monday	Jog two laps
	Stretch
	Sprint drills on grass
	Standing triple jumps into pit
	Approach runs on track
	Weights
Tuesday	Jog two laps
	Stretch
	Sprint drills on grass
	Standing triple jumps into pit
	Approach runs on track
	Four-step jumps
	Full approach jumps
Wednesday	Jog two laps
	Stretch
	Sprint drills on grass
	Standing triple jumps into pit
	Approach runs on track
	Weights
Thursday	Jog two laps
	Stretch
	Sprint drills on grass

	Standing triple jumps into pit
	Approach runs on track
	Four-step jumps
Friday	Competition or rest
Saturday	Competition or rest
Sunday	Rest

POLE VAULT

The pole vault is one of the most exciting spectator events in track and field. You do not have to understand all the intricacies to appreciate an athlete speeding down the runway with a pole more than twice her height, then flinging herself over a bar higher than a rooftop.

It's a dramatic event with obvious danger. People with a fear of heights should stay away from the pole vault. The event tends to attract daredevils who would be bored with many other events.

Pole vaulters need to be aggressive by nature. But they can't be reckless. Vaulters must respect the danger of the sport at all times and become grounded in the fundamentals before trying to clear great heights. Athletes must know their capabilities and limits and not impulsively try to exceed them. It's far better and safer to make gradual progress in the pole vault than to suddenly try to jump two feet higher than your previous best. If you do, you're setting yourself up for failure and possible injury.

Successful pole vaulters are among the best athletes in track and field. Consider the requirements: speed, strength, endurance, body control, fearlessness. Pole vaulters cannot be single-dimensional athletes. They often have the athletic ability to excel in many events, but they choose pole vaulting because of its excitement. Only vaulters know the rush of firmly planting the pole, feeling it bend in their hands, rising toward the bar feet-first, clearing the bar, then free-falling onto the mat as the pole falls to the ground. Exhilaration!

Women overcame one of the last obstacles in track and field when pole vaulting became an Olympic event for women in 2000. And why shouldn't it be? Men cannot have this thrilling event to themselves.

THE BASICS

- Just as in the high jump, competitors are eliminated after three consecutive failures at any height.
- The pole can be made of any material and be any length and diameter. The only requirement is that the surface must be smooth. Women vaulters often use poles that are about 15 feet long.

- In the early days of pole vaulting, athletes used wood poles. Bamboo came next, followed by aluminum. Fiberglass, the material of choice today, came into use about 40 years ago. Fiberglass is heavier than aluminum, but athletes prefer it because it has more spring and offers more propulsion over the bar.
- Competitors consider their height, weight, and speed in choosing the specifications of a pole.
- They are allowed to wrap up to two layers of adhesive tape around the pole and put rosin or other sticky substance on their hands for better grip.
- Athletes usually bring three poles to a meet to be prepared for different conditions such as high winds or rain.
- A broken pole does not constitute a foul. Fouls occur if a competitor doesn't clear the bar, knocks the bar off its supports, or places her lower hand above the upper hand while in the air.
- Vaulters forcefully put the pole in a metal box flush with the ground at the end of the runway. Then they begin their ascent to the bar.
- The bar is raised at least five centimeters after each round.
- Athletes may request that the standards, the supports for the crossbar, be moved slightly—less than a meter—toward the runway or toward the pit.
- Each competitor has two minutes to attempt her vault.

TECHNIQUE

To be successful in this event, athletes must first become comfortable carrying a pole. That's no small feat, especially considering the length of today's poles. New materials have made poles light enough that athletes can use poles 15 feet or longer.

As athletes in the long jump and high jump know, it's difficult enough making a smooth, accelerating approach with your hands empty. Add the challenge of toting a long pole, and many athletes are immediately excluded from this event: They cannot get the hang of it.

Planting the pole and clearing the bar are separate tasks with their own difficulties. Before yc⁻. can tackle those phases, you must master the approach. Once again, speed is king. If you don't achieve blazing speed as you approach the bar, there's no way you can clear a respectable height. More than in any other jumping event, success in the pole vaulting is tied to what you do on the ground.

Pole vaulters must be eager learners because the event has many complex elements. Most pole vaulters are naturally aggressive, but no one is born with a knowledge of vaulting mechanics. You must acquire that little by little. Be patient. Most great pole vaulters began at an early age because there's so much to learn. The earlier you start, the more time you have.

Grip and Pole Carry

Before working on the approach, athletes must learn to grip and carry the pole properly. Because of its length and weight, a strong grip is absolutely essential. Someone with powerful hands and arms is able to have a higher grip on the pole during the jump. The higher the grip, the higher you can vault.

Athletes can carry the pole on either side of their body, whichever is more comfortable and produces better faults. If you carry it on the right side, your left hand should be placed on top the pole. It should be about an inch above your waist and inch in front of your hips. By contrast, your right hand should be behind your hips toward the end of the pole. That hand is on the outside of the pole as if you're shaking hands with it. The two hands are about 18–30 inches apart.

Some athletes begin their approach run with the pole pointing almost straight at the sky. Others carry it at a 45-degree angle to the ground, while still others have it parallel to the ground. This is a matter of personal preference. The higher you carry the pole during the approach, the greater the wind resistance it will create. Also, it may be more difficult to lower the pole into the plant box and make a strong takeoff.

However, some vaulters think that carrying the pole higher feels more comfortable and lets them run faster during the approach and, thus, vault themselves higher. The higher you hold the pole, the lighter it tends to feel. To carry it high during the run-up, press down on the pole with your right hand. This forces the plant end up.

Proper method of carrying pole at start

Proper method of carrying pole during approach

Approach

The approach run should be 30 to 45 meters long. A longer run-up usually produces more speed. But it also can lead to an inconsistent stride pattern and deceleration.

If you carry the pole on your right side, start your approach with your left foot on the starting mark. This gives you a balanced feel. To begin, rock back slightly on your right foot, then push off powerfully with it.

As you approach the plant box, steadily increase your speed. Keep your body upright and shoulders square. Gradually lower the tip of the pole as you near the end of the runway and approach the plant box. Count your steps at first. Most vaulters take 15 to 20 strides. The more you rehearse your steps, the less likely you are to be indecisive and take stutter-steps as you near takeoff.

Pole Plant and Takeoff

The pole plant should become as automatic as the run-up. You want to instinctively plant the pole in the correct place, not look down and

Planting pole in box at end of runway

try to aim it into the box. If you do, you'll lose momentum and make a weak jump. The planting motion begins about three steps from the box. First, lower the tip of the pole below your waist, raising your right arm above your head (if you're carrying the pole on your right side). When you plant the pole, it should be directly above your jumping foot. Your eyes and chest need to point up and out. Your takeoff leg (the left leg in this case) straightens on the last step, as your right arm straightens overhead.

Now, press up on the pole—toward the pit—with your left hand. This bends the pole away from the bar. Your right arm, meanwhile, remains straight and high on the other end of the pole. As you push up on middle of the pole with your left hand and down on the end with

your right hand, you proper yourself upward.

Your feet rise first, and your body becomes vertical, upside down. The pole then straightens, pushing you closer and closer to the bar.

Clearing the Bar

When you reach the bar, rotate around the pole so that your stomach—not your back—faces the bar. Your feet and legs will clear first. Then, bend at the waist to let your upper body pass over. Once it has cleared, arch your back and push the pole away to complete the vault.

You've done it! Now relax and fall onto the mat. Be care-

In the air before and after clearing the bar

ful to land on your upper back and shoulder—not on your neck—to avoid injury.

RECORDS

WORLD RECORD

- 15'9.25" (Stacy Dragila—USA, 6/9/01)

U.S. NATIONAL RECORDS

- [ages 13–14]—10'6" (Jenny Green of Grand Island, Nebraska, 7/30/99)
- [ages 15–16]—12'5.5" (Julene Bailey of Nampa, Idaho, 7/5/01)
- [ages 17–18]—12'7.25" (Elizabeth Boyle of Chicago, Illinois, 7/28/01)

Source: USA Track & Field

FAULTS AND FIXES

Fault: After planting the pole, the athlete slows down as she rises in the air and fails to reach a vertical position.
Result: Can't achieve adequate height to clear bar.
Fix: Increase speed of approach. Without a fast run-up, the athlete won't achieve the momentum to reach a vertical position and gain enough height.

Fault: The upper arm is flexed, instead of straight, at takeoff.
Result: Loss of power on swing upward.
Fix: Try placing your right hand (for right-handed jumpers) higher on the pole during the approach run. This will force you to extend your right arm at takeoff and gain the necessary upward lift.

Fault: Athlete's chest hits pole during takeoff.
Result: Disrupts rhythm, prevents adequate height and clearance.
Fix: When the pole is planted, the athlete should push up on the pole firmly with the left arm. This lets the athlete rock back into the correct position.

Fault: Athlete's legs don't get high enough during the swing upward.
Result: Inability to clear bar.
Fix: Keep the right arm locked at takeoff, then drop the shoulders back and flex the legs at the knee. This allows the body to store enough power to elevate the legs vertically. Do not bend at the waist.

Fault: The pole doesn't flex enough during the swing.
Result: Pole can't catapult the athlete to an adequate height.
Fix: Check the pole. It may be too stiff for you. Try a more flexible pole. Also, check your hand position on the pole. They could be too low or too close together.

Fault: Athlete doesn't make the proper half-rotation around the pole as she nears the bar.
Result: Never achieves the face-down position on top of the bar that's needed for clearance.
Fix: Keep feet closer to the pole during the upward pull. This helps athlete retain momentum as she rises, allowing her to make the proper rotation for clearance.

DRILLS

Rope Climb

Find a gym that has a rope attached to the ceiling. Place your hands on the rope over your head and gradually pull yourself up. Continue until you can touch the ceiling. This drill produces great upper body strength and simulates the pull upward on the pole used in vaulting. [*Note: Be sure to have mats below you and someone assisting you. Don't go higher than you safely can.*]

Rope Swing

Use the same rope as above. Place your hands on the rope over your head. Jog about five steps, then swing your lower body up and drop your head and chest back. This simulates the vertical position during the lift phase of the pole vault.

Backward Handstand

Sit with your legs extended in front of you and hands on either side of your head, palms up. Roll backward on your shoulders and go into a handstand, raising your legs straight up and locking your arms. Have one or two spotters at your side to help you reach a vertical position. This drill simulates the upward drive on the pole that's necessary for clearance.

Swing and Rotate

Make a five-step approach run toward the pit, with your hands low on the pole. Plant the pole in the box, then swing your legs up and around the right side of the pole. At the same time, rotate your body a half-turn so that your eyes face the runway and you land on your feet on the mat. Don't let go of the pole. This drills develops the rhythm you need for vaulting.

Back Pushes

Prepare to make a vault at full speed. After you plant the pole and lean backward, a coach pushes firmly on your back. This assistance helps creates confidence to go higher and become more aggressive.

SAMPLE WORKOUTS

POLE VAULT (OFF-SEASON)	
Monday	Jog two laps Stretch Sprint drills on grass Ten 60-meter buildup runs Weights
Tuesday	Jog two laps Stretch Sprint drills on grass Pole runs Sliding box plants
Wednesday	Jog two laps Stretch Sprint drills on grass Ten 60-meter buildup runs Weights
Thursday	Jog two laps Stretch Sprint drills on grass Pole runs Sliding box plants
Friday	Jog two laps Stretch Sprint drills on grass Ten 60-meter buildup runs Weights
Saturday/Sunday	Rest

POLE VAULT (EARLY SEASON)	
Monday	Jog two laps Stretch Sprint drills on grass Pole runs Sliding box plants Weights
Tuesday	Jog two laps Stretch Sprint drills on grass Pole runs Pop ups Plant drills from four steps Six-step jumps
Wednesday	Jog two laps Stretch Sprint drills on grass Pole runs Sliding box plants Weights
Thursday	Jog two laps Stretch Sprint drills on grass Pole runs Pop ups Plant drills from four steps Six-step jumps Full run jumps (when ready)
Friday	Competition or rest
Saturday	Competition
Sunday	Rest

POLE VAULT (MID-SEASON)	
Monday	Jog two laps Stretch Sprint drills on grass Pole runs Six-step jumps Weights
Tuesday	Jog two laps Stretch Sprint drills on grass Pole runs Pop ups Plant drills from four steps

	Six-step jumps
	Full run jumps
Wednesday	Jog two laps
	Stretch
	Sprint drills on grass
	Pole runs
	Six-step jumps
	Weights
Thursday	Jog two laps
	Stretch
	Sprint drills on grass
	Pole runs
	Pop ups
	Plant drills from four steps
	Six-step jumps
	Full run jumps
Friday	Competition or rest
Saturday	Competition or rest
Sunday	Rest

SUPERSTAR: STACY DRAGILA

Stacy Dragila always liked track and field.

In high school in California, she competed in the hurdles and reached the state finals. At Idaho State University, she turned to the multi-event heptathlon.

Stacy did well, but it wasn't until her coach suggested that she try the pole vault in 1993 that she found her true calling. Only three years later, she won the U.S. Indoor and U.S. Outdoor championships in the pole vault, a relatively new event for women. She kept improving dramatically.

She has now won the World Championship twice and the U.S. Outdoor title six times. More importantly, she took the gold medal in the 2000 Olympics, the first time pole vaulting had been an Olympic event for women. She currently holds the world record of 15'9 1/4".

Stacy understands why some athletes are reluctant to try the pole vault. She started out with the bar at only 6 feet.

"The first couple trillion times trying to go over the bar were pretty frightening for me," she joked.

Before long, however, she overcame her fear and went on to international fame. Her determination has fueled her success.

"I always went after things that inspired me," Stacy said. "I was very goal-oriented and never let anybody get in my way."

7

THROWING EVENTS

The throwing events—shot put, discus, and javelin—may lack the glamour of running and jumping events, but they are challenging and enjoyable nonetheless.

These events demand not only upper body strength, but total body coordination. Even stout shot putters are usually good athletes. Many young people who are simply big don't have the body control, flexibility, and timing to heave a shot put, hurl a discus, or launch a javelin.

Of the three throwing events, athletes in the shot put and discus tend to be the most similar. Normally, they are muscular and hefty. However, it's still possible to do well in the shot and discus without being large. If you have adequate strength and combine it with excellent technique, you can beat many bigger girls.

The javelin, in particular, does not require an athlete to have a certain physique. Some top female javelin throwers are tall and lean, while others are short and muscular. The javelin depends less on brute strength and more on a fluid, precisely timed approach run and explosive release.

The javelin throw is a dramatic event to watch. Spectators and competitors get to watch the spear rise against the sky, reach an apex and then dive into the ground. You can try to guess how far the javelin will travel based on its initial path.

More people should appreciate the throwing events. Competitors certainly respect one another. They know the skill and dedication it takes to be a winner in the shot put, discus, and javelin. Success comes from hours of practice, often alone. Throwers often find themselves in one corner of the workout area, away from athletes in the more popular running and jumping events.

Throwing events illustrate, once again, the many facets of track and field and why the sport is so appealing. Athletes who dominate in running and jumping events probably won't dominate in throwing events. The shot put, javelin, and discus allow girls who can't necessarily leap high or run faster than everyone else to shine. For some girls, the throws turn out to be their thing.

SHOT PUT

The shot put is about the size of a softball. But try picking one up. You certainly won't mistake it for a softball then. In high school, the shot put weighs four kilograms, which is heavier than it might sound.

Because of the shot put's weight, athletes need at least average strength and preferably more. If you start with a base of strength and add proper throwing technique, you're likely to do well.

Two methods are used to throw the shot put. Top throwers have used both with success. The oldest style, called the glide, is easier to learn and often leads to more consistent results. The other, the spin, is more complex but is more effective for some people. The choice is yours. Try both and then decide. Whichever you choose, you need to have smooth, balanced motion to get the greatest distance.

THE BASICS

- The shot put is smooth and round and made of iron, brass, or another solid metal. In high school competition, the girls' shot put weighs four kilograms.
- The shot put is thrown from a concrete circle that is 2.1 meters, or seven feet, in diameter.
- The ring is bounded by a band of metal. A raised piece of wood or metal at the front of the circle is called a stopboard. An athlete's foot may rest against the stopboard, but not be on top of it. The stopboard is intended to provide support for your foot as you make the throw.
- The shot put is thrown into a fan-shaped area that gets wider further from the throwing circle. The end of the landing area is about 30 meters from the circle.
- Officials raise a red flag to indicate a foul. That means the athlete stepped on the stopboard or outside of the circle or the shot put landed outside the marked area. A white flag indicates a legal throw.
- Athletes have a minute and a half to make their throw.
- They're not allowed to wear gloves, but they can apply an approved sticky substance to their hands to improve their grip.

- Competitors may wear wide athletic belts to protect their backs from injury.

TECHNIQUE

Glide

Coaches usually teach beginning shot putters the glide first. Besides being simpler to learn, it lets a young athlete understand the fundamentals of throwing the shot put. Even athletes who later advance to the spin method are better off by learning the glide. In fact, some of the world's best shot putters try the spin but come back to the glide.

To start your throw, face the back of the circle away from where you will throw. Place all your weight on your right foot (assuming you're right-handed). Flex your right knee and bend at the waist so that your upper body is almost parallel to the ground. Hold the shot put with your middle three fingers and thumb. Rest it against the right side of your neck, under your jaw. Your left arm points down and back to keep you balanced.

Now, push firmly off your right leg while kicking your left leg toward the front of the circle. (This is the *glide.*) Your hips should turn more than your upper body at first. This tension between your upper body and lower body creates the power necessary for a long throw.

At this point, most of your weight is still on your right leg and the shot put is still against your neck. Now, begin to unwind your body toward the front of the ring. When you reach the two o'clock position (the top of the circle being 12 o'clock), start the throwing motion. Push up forcefully with your legs. Thrust the shot away from your neck. Fully extend your right arm and let the shot roll off your fingertips. It should start off at a 40-degree angle to the ground. Be sure to keep your head up and chest forward as you complete the throw.

Once the shot put is gone, you should be standing flat-footed on your right leg at the top of the circle. Your left leg points behind you and is hip-high to keep you balanced. Allow your momentum to carry you to the left until you come to a stop at about nine o'clock.

Spin

Once you're comfortable with the glide method, you can try the spin. However, if you're comfortable with the glide and are having good results, you can certainly stick with it.

The spin resembles the throwing motion for the discus. You spin one and a half times around the circle before throwing the shot put. In

Glide method: Progress from start (facing rear of ring) to finish after release, standing on one foot

the glide, by contrast, you make a more compact move straight to the front of the circle.

To start your throw using the spin, stand at the rear of the circle with your feet slightly wider than your shoulders. Bend your knees slightly and keep your upper body erect. Your right foot should be flat against the ground.

Twist the left side of your body—arm, knee and shoulder—slightly to the right (clockwise). This is a preliminary move in the opposite

Spin method: Progress from start to finish

direction of the throwing motion. It helps you creates power and momentum for the throw.

Next, lift your right foot off the ground and drive your right shoulder to the left (counterclockwise) toward the front of the circle. Your body unwinds, and your weight shifts to your left foot. Continue to spin around the circle, and let your weight move back to your right leg. Keep going. Both feet should reach the top of the circle at the same time. Now, drive your legs up strongly, push the shot put away from your neck, straighten your right arm and release the shot off your fingertips.

Just as in the glide, your momentum will carry you to the left, to about nine o'clock. Some throwers spin even further around after throwing, until they face the back of the circle. If you've kept your balance after the throw, and not fallen to one side or the other, you've probably made a good throw.

RECORDS

WORLD RECORD

- 74'3" (Natalya Lisovskaya—Soviet Union, 6/7/87)

U.S. NATIONAL RECORDS

- [ages 13–14; using 6-pound shot]—52'1$\frac{1}{4}$" (Susie Ray of Orange, California, 1976)
- [ages 15–16; using 4-kilogram shot]—49'10$\frac{1}{2}$" (Michelle Carter of Ovilla, Texas, 7/27/01)
- [ages 17–18; using 4-kilogram shot]—51'1$\frac{3}{4}$" (Michelle Carter of Ovilla, Texas, 7/27/02)

Source: USA Track & Field

FAULTS AND FIXES

Fault: Athlete loses her balance during the throwing motion.
Result: Doesn't establish proper throwing position, makes weak throw.
Fix: Work on technique, concentrating on body position and footwork from start to finish. Keep your head level with the horizon.

Fault: Athlete falls backward while making throw.
Result: Short throw.
Fix: Improve thrust from legs and hips, don't try to throw with your arms alone. Make sure chest is moving up and out as you throw.

Fault: Athlete releases the shot put from the palm, instead of letting it roll off the fingertips.
Result: Shortened distance.
Fix: Check grip. Shot put should be held against the pads of your fingers and thumbs, then move to the fingertips for the throw. Practice your throws while standing in place. Be sure to extend your arm and fingers fully.

Fault: The shot put is released too low.
Result: Lack of distance.

Fix: Raise your throwing arm. Improve the thrust with your legs, hips, arms and chest at release.

Fault: Shot put goes sideways and lands outside the marked area.
Result: Foul. Throw doesn't count.
Fix: Be sure to move forward—do not continue to spin sideways—as you throw the shot. If you don't learn to end your spin motion at the top of the circle, you'll continue to throw the shot put to the side.

SUCCESS STORY: MICHELLE CARTER

Michelle Carter, a record-setting high school shot putter in Texas, had a great coach when she was starting out: her dad, Michael Carter.

He won a silver medal in the 1984 Olympics and later was an all-pro defensive lineman for the San Francisco 49ers.

Despite his fame, he never pushed his eldest daughter into track. She says it was her idea to pick up the shot put for the first time when she was 12 years old.

"He doesn't want us to think about what he did," said Michelle, who now attends the University of Texas on a track scholarship. "He wants us to think about what we can do."

And she has done a lot. During her high school career in the Dallas area, Michelle won three straight state titles in the shot put while setting a state record. Her record compares favorably to her father's accomplishments. He set state and national records high school records in the shot put in the late 1970s.

She said she has become accustomed to comparisons to her father. But she says she doesn't mind.

"Sure, he did what he did," Michelle said. "But I know him as my dad."

Michael Carter, understandably, is a proud father. When Michelle was still in high school, she placed third in the U.S. Junior Nationals while competing against college athletes.

"Time will tell how good she is," Michael said. "She has to continue to work and learn."

That shouldn't be a problem. Michelle is a dedicated athlete, just as her father was.

She's got her eye on the 2004 Olympics.

"My daddy could beat anybody," Michelle said. "It's in my blood, but I do what I do. I just want to be the best."

DRILLS

Simple Lift

Stand and hold a shot put in your throwing hand next to your jaw. Slowly extend your arm, and the shot put, straight up. Get used to the weight and feel of it. Repeat 10 times. Once you become comfortable lifting the shot put, you're ready to work on the throwing motion.

Wrist Flips

Stand and hold a shot put next to your jaw. Gradually extend your arm up and out about 45 degrees. When your arm is straight, gently flip the shot put off your fingertips. This simulates the proper release motion. Repeat five times. Be careful not to drop the shot put on your foot.

Basketball Throws Against a Wall

Stand six feet from a gym wall with the basketball in your right hand (for right-handed throwers). Take a step forward with your left leg, then step forward with your right leg and toss the basketball at a 45-degree angle firmly against the wall. Note the ball flight. Catch the ball as it rebounds off the wall. Repeat twice. This drills lets you feel the upper body muscles involved in throwing the shot put.

Simple lift: While standing, she starts with the shot against her jaw, then raises it straight up

Wrist flips: Similar to end of actual throw, extend throwing arm and flip the shot over the fingertips

Basketball Throws for Distance

Go to an open field. This drill is the same as the one above, except that you throw the ball as far as you can down the field, not against a wall. Again, feel your upper body muscles and watch the ball leave your hand at a 45-degree angle.

Shot Put from Standing Position

In this drill, you use a shot put. Stand in a throwing circle, facing backward (six o'clock) about two steps from the top of the circle. Get in the proper starting position, with the shot put against your neck and jaw. Flex both knees and place all your weight on your right foot. Bend at the waist so that your upper body is almost parallel to the ground. Now, push off firmly with your right leg, kick your left leg toward the outside of the circle and plant it at the top. Unwind your body, place your right foot near the stopboard and release the shot put. Extend your chest and arm and let the shot put roll off your fingertips. Repeat twice.

Gliding Practice

In this drill, you don't use a shot put or any other object. The purpose is to work on your throwing form. The windup needs to become second nature, or you won't make consistent throws. Get in the starting position described above. However, begin at the back of the circle. Place your weight on your right foot and extend your left leg behind you toward the top of the circle. Keep your body low and glide backward, leading with your left leg. When you get to the top of the circle, plant your left foot firmly, face straight ahead and release the shot put. Repeat this drill twice.

SAMPLE WORKOUTS

SHOT PUT (OFF-SEASON)	
Monday	Jog and stretch Weights (medicine ball drills)
Tuesday	Jog and stretch Single-leg hops Double-leg hops Ten 30-meter dashes
Wednesday	Jog and stretch Weights (medicine ball drills)
Thursday	Jog and stretch Single-leg hops Double-leg hops Ten 30-meter dashes
Friday	Jog and stretch Weights (medicine ball drills)
Saturday/Sunday	Rest

SHOT PUT (EARLY SEASON AND MID-SEASON)	
Monday	Jog and stretch Standing throws Work on footwork Weights (medicine ball drills)
Tuesday	Jog and stretch Standing throws Work on footwork Power position throws Full throws

SHOT PUT (EARLY SEASON AND MID-SEASON) *(continued)*	
Wednesday	Jog and stretch
	Standing throws
	Work on footwork
	Power position throws
	Weights (medicine ball drills)
Thursday	Jog and stretch
	Standing throws
	Work on footwork
	Power position throws
	Full throws
Friday	Competition or rest
Saturday	Competition or rest
Sunday	Rest

DISCUS

Unlike the shot put, there's only one effective throwing technique for the discus. It's a rotary motion, similar to the spin method in the shot put. You make almost two complete turns around the circle before letting go of the discus.

This event requires great strength, speed, and balance. Top discus throwers are often tall, rangy athletes. A person with long arms and arms can build up tremendous acceleration as she spins around the circle, producing a long throw.

Spectators may focus on the athlete's arm as she throws the discus. But a good throw requires the total body action. If you try to simply rely on arm strength, you won't be successful and you may injure yourself.

Some people make the mistake of comparing the discus throw to tossing a Frisbee. Both objects have the same general shape, but the comparison ends there. A Frisbee is so light that you can flip it with only a slight movement of the wrist. To throw the heavier discus, you have to build up momentum using your entire body.

THE BASICS

- The discus is normally made of wood. It has a smooth metal rim around the exterior and metal plates in the center.
- In high school, the girls' discus weighs one kilogram.
- The discus is thrown from a circle that is two meters in diameter, slightly larger than the shot put ring. The discus ring, unlike the shot put ring, does not have a stopboard.

- The throwing circle is surrounded by a tall protective cage to prevent errant throws from hitting somebody.
- Contestants throw the discus into a fan-shaped area that widens away from the throwing circle. It's about 100 meters long.
- An official raises a white flag if the throw is legal and a red flag if there's a foul. A foul occurs if an athlete steps beyond the throwing circle or the discus doesn't land in the marked area.

TECHNIQUE

Grip

Proper grip

A good throw begins with the proper grip. The edge of the discus should rest against the inside of your four fingers, near the end of the fingers. Most throwers spread their fingers slightly to get a more stable grip. However, you want to hold the discus lightly. It might surprise you, but a long throw can only be made with a light grip. Light pressure allows your arm to stay loose and whip the discus down the field.

Your grip pressure should be so light, in fact, that the discus would fall to the ground if you were walking. The force during the throwing motion holds the discus in place.

Set-Up and Throw

Spread your feet about shoulder-width and face the back of the circle (the six o'clock position). Your right foot is flat on the ground (for a right-handed thrower) and your left foot rests on the balls of the foot.

Begin with a reverse move to your right, just as in the spin method for the shot put. Do this by twisting your upper body and letting your right arm (and discus) go far behind your back. Then, move your torso back to the left and shift your weight onto the ball of your left foot. Your right foot now leaves the ground and begins a wide sweep around the outer edge of the circle.

Keep your shoulders level and left arm extended in front of you to stay in balance. As you rotate around the ring, drive off your left leg and pull your right leg across body while bent at a 90-degree angle. This helps you spin faster.

When you go past the top of the circle, place all your weight on the ball of your right foot. Raise your left foot. Be sure to keep both arms relaxed and parallel to the ground.

Continue spinning to the left, with your body low to the ground. Your left leg should reach the top of the circle first. Keep your right arm (and discus) behind your upper body to build up maximum force. Then, drop your right arm, raise your shoulders toward the top of the circle and release the discus from the two o'clock position. Tilt your head back to let your chest and hips rise during release. The discus should come off the outside of your index finger at a 20-degree angle to the ground. It will spin counterclockwise.

Throwing motion begins with reverse move

Progression from start to finish (above and opposite)

After the throw, kick your left leg behind you and hop sideways on your right foot to keep you from moving forward and across the line. That's a foul.

RECORDS

WORLD RECORD
- 252' (Gabriele Reinsch—East Germany, 7/9/88)

U.S. NATIONAL RECORDS
- [ages 13–14]—152' (Suzy Powell of Modesto, California, 6/23/90)
- [ages 15–16]—164'5" (Elizabeth Debartolo of Aurora, Illinois, 5/12/97)
- [ages 17–18]—175'3" (Suzy Powell of Modesto, California, 7/9/95)

Source: USA Track & Field

FAULTS AND FIXES

Fault: Athlete releases discus from the back of the hand, instead of the index finger.
Result: Weak throw.
Fix: Understand proper throwing technique. To generate proper power, discus must come off the front of the hand. Practice standing throws. Make sure throwing arm is extended at release, not bent at the elbow. Practice bowling with the discus, rolling it off your index finger.

Fault: Throwing arm doesn't stay behind the body.
Result: Athlete doesn't store enough power.
Fix: Work on technique until you can feel the proper position for your arm. When your arm is extended behind you until the last moment, you can whip the discus down the field. Try throwing a plastic cone to feel the resistance. Make sure your elbow isn't bent or your arm isn't pointing to the side when you throw.

Fault: Athlete's upper body turns too soon toward the front of the circle.
Result: Improper throwing position, discus goes sideways instead of straight ahead.
Fix: Coordinate movement of upper and lower body during windup. Legs and hips should reach the top of the circle before the upper body to ensure a good throw.

Fault: Throwing arm is too low, around the knee, when the discus is released.

Result: High, short throw.

Fix: Practice proper form. Arm should be almost parallel to ground to make a strong throw that gradually rises.

DRILLS

Arm Swing

Stand with your throwing arm extended out to the side and a discus in hand. Keep your arm parallel to the ground and move it forward and backward in a smooth motion. Get used to the feel of the discus. Keep the rest of your body still. Repeat a dozen times.

Sitting Throw

Sit with your legs in front of you and flared out in a V. Hold a basketball in your right hand (for the right-handed thrower). Bring the ball as far as possible behind your back, then swing your arm forward and toss the ball up and out. This drill simulates the throwing motion for the discus. Repeat three times.

Step and Sling

Get a small rubber ring about three feet in diameter. (You can make one from a garden hose). Stand in a discus ring facing backward. Place your weight on your right foot. Swing the ring as far as possible behind your right shoulder. Turn your body and bring your left foot forward, placing it at the top of the ring. Step forward with your right foot and toss the ring down the field. Repeat three times.

Complete Throw with Rubber Ring

Stand at the rear of the throwing circle, facing backward. Make a complete windup and throw, as if you were holding a discus. By using the lighter rubber ring, you're able to focus on proper body position, footwork and arm extension. Repeat twice.

Spin Practice

Face to the side and hold a discus in your right hand behind you. Keep your arm low. Step forward and turn your shoulders 90 degrees until you face straight ahead. Squeeze the discus with your little finger and let it roll along your fingers and come off your index finger. Straighten your arm as you release it. The discus will spin clockwise. Learn to feel the correct release technique. Repeat twice.

SAMPLE WORKOUTS

DISCUS (OFF-SEASON, EARLY SEASON, AND MID-SEASON)	
Monday	Jog and stretch Weights (medicine ball drills)
Tuesday	Jog and stretch Single-leg hops Double-leg hops Ten 30-meter dashes
Wednesday	Jog and stretch Weights (medicine ball drills)
Thursday	Jog and stretch Single-leg hops Double-leg hops Ten 30-meter dashes
Friday	Jog and stretch Weights (medicine ball drills)
Saturday/Sunday	Rest

DISCUS (EARLY SEASON AND MID-SEASON)	
Monday	Jog and stretch Standing throws Work on footwork Weights (medicine ball drills)
Tuesday	Jog and stretch Standing throws Work on footwork Power position throws Full throws
Wednesday	Jog and stretch Standing throws Work on footwork Power position throws Weights (medicine ball drills)
Thursday	Jog and stretch Standing throws Work on footwork Power position throws Full throws
Friday	Competition or rest
Saturday	Competition or rest
Sunday	Rest

JAVELIN

The javelin throw has had to change with the times. As athletes have become bigger and stronger, throws have gotten longer and longer. Officials became concerned that athletes were launching the javelin *too far*. They worried about the safety of spectators and other athletes who were watching the competition. Naturally, if a person doesn't get out of the way of a falling javelin, they can be hurt seriously or even killed.

So, periodically, governing officials have ordered changes to the balance point of the javelin, meaning where the athlete grips the javelin. By moving the grip only slightly one way or the other, the height and length of the throw can be changed dramatically.

Still, many states don't allow the javelin throw in high school out of concern for safety. Even with a javelin that doesn't go as far, some school officials don't think they can guarantee the safety of onlookers.

If your state permits the javelin (ask your coach), it's a fun and challenging event to try. It requires a speedy approach run and explosiveness at release. You'll enjoy seeing the javelin sail further and further as your technique improves.

Even if your state does not allow high school javelin competition, you might have an opportunity to try it in college. So you could become acquainted with the fundamentals now.

THE BASICS

- The runway for the approach is 30 to 36 meters long. Contestants are allowed to place marks where they want to begin running and where they will start the throwing motion.
- At the end of the runway, there's a metal or wood arc or stopboard eight meters long. Contestants must not cross that stopboard or they commit a foul.
- The javelin is thrown into a fan-shaped area. The far end is about 100 meters from the stopboard.
- The javelin must land tip-first to be a legal throw, but it does not have to stick into the ground.
- For females of all ages, the javelin weighs 600 grams and is 7'2$\frac{1}{2}$" to 7'6$\frac{1}{2}$". It is made of metal or wood.

TECHNIQUE
Grip

The correct grip is critical just as in the shot put and discus. Never carelessly pick up a javelin and throw it. For one thing, it could easily go awry and hurt someone.

Grip, first style

Grip, second style

The javelin has a non-slip, corded grip near the mid-point. That's where you hold it. Three different finger grips can be used. In the first, all four fingers are placed on the top of the javelin, and it rests in the palm of the hand. The second is the same, except that the index finger points backwards. In the third grip, rarely used today, the javelin sits in the gap between your index and middle fingers—in the V. Your palm faces forward as you throw, and your other three fingers curl around the top of the javelin.

Grip, third style

Approach and Throw

Like the grip, the approach is vital. You want to build up as much *controllable* speed as possible to make a long throw. If you run too fast, you can get out of sync or decelerate, and your throwing technique will suffer. You need to gradually build speed as you near the end of the runway.

Most athletes take 12 to 15 steps during the approach, although some use only eight to 10. This is up to you. If you're not sure how many to take, start out with fewer steps until you feel comfortable enough to make a longer approach.

During the run-up, keep your upper body and shoulders relaxed and the javelin resting comfortably in your hand. It takes practice to run smoothly while holding a javelin. The tip of the javelin should point down slightly during the approach. Look straight ahead and keep your shoulders and hips square.

During the last five steps of the approach, you prepare to make your throw. Begin by stepping with your left foot (for a right-handed thrower) and turning your shoulders to the right. Bring your arm as far as possible behind your back. Your hand needs to be slightly above your shoulder and javelin even with your eyes. Extend your left arm forward and across your chest for balance.

On the next-to-last step, your left foot should land flat against the runway and straighten. Now lean your upper body back. To start your

Approach run

Javelin released overhead

After release, balancing on left leg and foot

throw, swing your right leg forward with the knee bent and toes pointing up. Drive off your left foot and thrust your torso and arm up and out. Keep your right arm loose to allow you to whip the javelin forward.

At release, the javelin should be above your head and leave your hand at a 35-degree angle. Make sure your right foot lands behind the foul line.

RECORDS

WORLD RECORD

- 234'8" (Osleidys Menéndez—Cuba, 7/1/01)

U.S. NATIONAL RECORDS

- [ages 13–14]—124'5" (Julie Butler of West Lake, Louisiana, 7/28/02)
- [ages 15–16]—152'8" (Rachel Walker of Benton, Louisiana, 7/29/00)
- [ages 17–18]—158'7$^{1}/_{2}$" (Sarah Malone of Newburg, Oregon, 7/24/99)

FAULTS AND FIXES

Fault: Athlete doesn't lean backward before release. Instead, body remains upright.
Result: Weak throw, relying only on arm strength instead of entire body.
Fix: Work on approach and getting into throwing position. Feel the power you create as you arch backward and extend the javelin far behind you before release.

Fault: Right leg (for right-handed throwers) doesn't step in front of the left foot at release.
Result: Weak throw, don't use entire body for power.
Fix: Practice footwork during approach, particularly the last five steps. Mark off those steps and rehearse them over and over. As you release the javelin, extend your right foot in front of your body and to the left for added power. Your foot should come down near the stopboard.

Fault: The athlete carries the javelin too loosely.
Result: The tip points to the left or right of the proper release area, causing inaccurate throw and possible fouls.
Fix: Work on grip. Hold javelin firmly, but keep hands and arm relaxed. The tip should be eye-level during the approach.

Fault: Athlete releases the javelin with a sidearm motion, instead of directly overhead.
Result: Javelin goes too far left or right, loses distance.
Fix: Work on proper form. Make sure you're extending your right arm straight back before you throw. The tip should face the throwing area to ensure a straight throw.

Fault: Javelin is released with the tip too high.
Result: Javelin quickly falls to the ground too soon.
Fix: Practice proper release angle. Don't let the back tip of the javelin touch the ground before throw—that means the front end is too high. The tip should be at eye-level at release, not above your head.

DRILLS

Basketball Throw

Get on your knees, with your upper body erect. Hold a basketball overhead with your arms fully extended. Lean your upper body back as far as possible. Then bring your arms forward firmly and release the ball. This drill simulates the pulling sensation when the javelin is behind your head.

Basketball throw

Step and Throw

Stand with your arms extended overhead and a basketball in your hands. Step forward with your left foot, then your right and toss the ball forward with both hands.

Four-Step Throw

In this drill, use a softball. Stand with the ball in your right hand and your arm extended behind you. Straighten your left arm in front. Step forward with your left foot, then the right, then again with your left. Make a final step forward with your right foot while throwing the softball overhead.

Step and throw (above and right)

Standing Throw with a Javelin

Place your left foot forward, with the javelin in your right hand behind your shoulder. The tip of the javelin should be at eye-level and face up at 45 degrees. Step forward with your right foot and throw the javelin as far as possible. Be sure to extend your chest and arm fully.

Standing throw with javelin (above and following page)

Five-Step Throw with Javelin

This drill is like an actual throw, except that the approach is only five steps. The shorter run-up allows you to focus on the throwing motion that starts during the final steps.

SAMPLE WORKOUTS

	JAVELIN (OFF-SEASON)
Monday	Jog two laps as a warm-up Stretch Sprint drills on grass Ten 60-meter buildup runs Weights
Tuesday	Jog two laps as a warm-up Stretch Sprint drills on grass Single-leg hops Lunges Bench hops Hurdle hops
Wednesday	Jog two laps Stretch Sprint drills on grass Ten 60-meter buildup runs Weights

Thursday	Jog two laps Stretch Sprint drills on grass Single-leg hops Lunges Bench hops Hurdle hops
Friday	Jog two laps Stretch Sprint drills on grass Ten 60-meter buildup runs Weights
Saturday/Sunday	Rest

JAVELIN (EARLY SEASON AND MID-SEASON)

Monday	Jog two laps Stretch Sprint drills on grass Five-step throws Practice crossover steps at end of approach (don't throw the javelin) Weights
Tuesday	Jog two laps Stretch Sprint drills on grass Standing throws, starting with javelin behind head Three-step throws
Wednesday	Jog two laps Stretch Sprint drills on grass Five-step throws Practice crossover steps at end of approach (don't throw the javelin) Weights
Thursday	Jog two laps Stretch Sprint drills on grass Standing throws, starting with javelin behind head Three-step throws
Friday	Competition or rest
Saturday	Competition
Sunday	Rest

8

HEPTATHLON, CROSS-COUNTRY, MARATHON, AND TRIATHLON

So far, this book has discussed only traditional events that are part of the spring track and field season.

However, several other running events have gained popularity in recent years that aren't as common, or that fall outside of the usual definition of track and field. These are heptathlon, cross-country, marathon, and triathlon. Of the three, cross-country is by far the most popular in high school. Few schools offer the heptathlon. It's mainly a summer event sponsored by track clubs. Marathons and triathlons normally involve older competitors and are rarely sanctioned by schools.

Cross-country competitions are held in the fall, several months before the start of the spring track season. Middle- and long-distance track athletes often take part in cross-country because it provides excellent training and conditioning for track events. Cross-country races vary widely in length and set up. They are held away from a track, usually on a course that includes hills, fields, and varied terrain.

A few athletes get involved in marathons and triathlons while still in school, but most people turn to them once they're older. Still, there's no reason not to try a marathon or triathlon if you're properly conditioned, and they don't conflict with your school track season. Be sure to check with your coach first. He or she may not want you to expend the energy it takes for a marathon or triathlon if you're training for a school meet. Often, marathons and triathlons are held in the summer so that might be the time to try one if you're up for the challenge.

First we'll discuss the heptathlon. This consists of seven individual events—three running, two jumping and two throwing—that are held over two days. Heptathlons are more common in college than in high school, although they are gaining popularity in some parts of the country for teens. As you can imagine, the heptathlon is a supreme test of athletic skill and stamina.

HEPTATHLON

Many people had never heard of the heptathlon until the mid-1980s when Jackie Joyner-Kersee dominated the event. She won the silver medal in the 1984 Olympics, followed by gold medals in the 1988 and 1992 Olympics.

Jackie illustrates the type of all-around athlete that usually excels in the heptathlon. She led her Illinois high school basketball team to the state championship and won a basketball scholarship to UCLA, an athletic powerhouse, where she was a four-year starter and an all-American.

Her strongest individual event was the long jump. She was ranked number one in the world during her prime and could have dominated the long jump for years if she had focused solely on it. But Jackie did well in other events, and her decision to compete in the heptathlon was a good one. She achieved greater fame, and she helped popularize the heptathlon.

Every track coach would like to have a young Jackie Joyner-Kersee—someone who is outstanding in running, jumping, and throwing. But even Jackie had to work long and hard on the fundamentals of each event to be a champion. She'll tell you it takes hours and hours of practice, even years, to master the seven events that make up the heptathlon.

Traditionally, the heptathlon has attracted girls who excel in running or jumping events. But in other countries, heptathlon competitors are recruited from the throwing ranks.

Even Jackie Joyner-Kersee's best event was the long jump, she was more than adequate in the shot put and discus. For instance, her personal bests in the shot put (55 feet, 3 inches) and javelin (164 feet, 5 inches) stack up well against heptathlon athletes who had specialized in throwing events.

Top heptathletes are better in some events than others, but they rarely do poorly in any of the seven events. It's the job of a coach and the athlete to work on the weaker events to improve her chances of winning.

Training methods vary widely. If a girl is relatively weak in the throwing events, her workout might resemble that of a shot put or discus thrower. That is, she might do extra strength work. On the other hand, if an athlete struggles in running and jumping events, her regimen might be similar to a sprinter or high jumper, with more running and speed work.

All heptathletes, regardless of their strengths and weaknesses, need a varied, strenuous workout program to prepare for the demanding two-day heptathlon competition. Some heptathlon athletes train year around and they never take an extended time off. The reason is that it takes a lot of practice to master the technical elements of each event.

Mental, as well as physical, strength is vital in the heptathlon. Because the competition lasts two days, athletes must stay focused while they wait for their next event, and be ready to perform after a long delay. Heptathletes have to be prepared to go from running to jumping to throwing events. To do so, you must remain mentally sharp.

THE BASICS

- The heptathlon consists of seven events held over two days. The events on the first day are 100-meter hurdles, high jump, shot put, and 200 meters. The second-day events are long jump, javelin, and 800 meters.
- Athletes must participate in all events or be disqualified.
- Competitors earn points in each event based on their performance. The heptathlon winner is the one with the most points.
- The maximum number of points that can be accumulated is 9,971. The long jump offers the most points (1,520), followed by shot put and javelin (1,500 each), high jump (1,498), 100-meter hurdles (1,361), 200 meters (1,342), and 800 meters (1,250).
- Each day of competition can take eight to 10 hours.
- The heptathlon became an Olympic event for women in 1984. For the previous 20 years, women had competed in the pentathlon. It consisted of five events: 80-meter hurdles, shot put, high jump, long jump, and 200 meters.

She said it . . .

Jackie Joyner-Kersee is known as the greatest heptathlon athlete of all time. She's also adept at giving interesting, inspiring quotations. Here's a sampling:

- "For me, the challenge is to try to beat myself or do better than I did in the past. I try to keep in mind not what I have accomplished, but what I have to try to accomplish in the future."
- "I don't have to be enemies with someone to compete with them."
- "Jumping has always been the thing for me. It's like leaping for joy."
- "I see elegance and beauty in every female athlete."

SUCCESS STORY: DIANA AND JULIE PICKLER

A few years ago Diana and Julie Pickler had never heard of the heptathlon. Today, the identical twins are nationally ranked in the event at Washington State University.

When Diana and Julie entered a Dallas-area high school, they excelled in the 400 meters. Then a coach at another school suggested that they try the heptathlon because of their size (5'9", 135 pounds) and all-around athletic ability.

The sisters immediately fell in love with the hep, as they call it. Both had been involved in athletics all their lives, starting with gymnastics in grade school, and liked the challenge of competing in the varied heptathlon events.

"It really tests you," said Diana.

Her sister says, "It takes a whole different mentality to be a heptathlete."

"It's hard to find people who want to put the time into it," Julie said.

Diana and Julie usually arrive at workouts before athletes in other events and stay longer than most.

"It takes a lot of dedication and patience and drive," said Diana, 20, who is four minutes older than her sister. "There's always room for improvement. You've got to be serious and completely committed."

The twin's high school didn't offer the heptathlon, so they took part in summer club meets sponsored by USA Track & Field, the governing body for the sport. During the school track season, Diana and Julie competed in the individual events that make up the heptathlon.

Only two years after beginning the hep, the twins were nationally ranked among high school girls. As seniors, Julie won first place in the U.S. Junior National Championship, and Diana finished a close second. They say they are close, despite being each other's top opponent. Theirs is a friendly rivalry.

"It doesn't matter who wins—as long as one of us gets first and one gets second," Julie said.

When they graduated from high school in 2002, they could choose from a number of scholarship offers in the heptathlon. They wanted to go to the same school, and they agreed on Washington State.

Before starting college, Diana and Julie traveled to Jamaica for the World Junior Track and Field Championships. Neither finished among the leaders, but the experience competing in

(continued)

(continued)

another country against world-class athletes fueled their interest in the heptathlon.

"That was awesome," Julie said.

In their dorm room, they have a poster of Jackie Joyner-Kersee, the most famous heptathlete of all time. They also would like to bring home Olympic medals. They're aiming for the 2004 Olympics but say they may have a better chance in 2008 because they'll have more experience.

"That's probably our best shot," Diana said. "It takes several years to reach your peak. I've heard that many people peak at about 26."

For now, Julie and Diana are concentrating on their college career, trying to win conference championships and achieve all-American honors. They say they're glad they discovered the heptathlon and encourage young girls to try it.

"It's *my* thing," Julie said. "I'll never stop doing the heptathlon."

Cross-Country

Cross-country is more popular than some people realize and is becoming more so all the time. For instance, cross-country is the sixth-most popular girls' sport, according to the National Federation of High School Coaches and more than 160,000 girls take part in it each year, more than those involved in tennis or swimming.

Many athletes who run cross-country in the fall do so as a warm-up for the spring track season. But some athletes stay with it year around. They like the longer, varied courses, versus the repetition of running lap after lap on a track.

Long ago, cross-country was an Olympic sport for men but not for women. It was included in the 1912, 1920, and 1924 Olympics, but was then dropped because it wasn't considered suitable for the hot weather that often accompanies the Summer Games.

In 1962, the International Amateur Athletic Federation, which governs track and field worldwide, began sanctioning cross-country meets and establishing standards for men and women. The rules are less rigid than in track and field events. For women, cross-country courses are usually at least three miles, although formally there are no set distances. Because of the different lengths and makeups of courses, no national or world records are kept in cross-country.

Team competition is a big part of cross-country, particularly in high school. Teams consist of five to nine runners, and points are awarded by order of finish. For instance, a runner gets one point for finishing first, two for second, and so on. The team with the lowest score wins the competition.

Even though cross-country events are held in the fall, successful athletes usually train year around. People drawn to it normally love to run so coaches don't have to motivate them. If you're one of these people who like to run regardless of the weather or time of year, then cross-country might be for you.

However, take advantage of a good coach. He or she can guide your training to help you achieve the greatest success. Some people think that the more miles you run in training, the better you'll do in a cross-country meet. That's not necessarily so. Distance work is obviously important, but so is intelligence and a plan. It's possible—even common—to overtrain. If you run too many miles, you can break down your body and not be at your best for a meet. A coach can be helpful in assisting you in determine how strenuous to make your workouts.

Many cross-country athletes are thin, but they still need to be strong. Weight training is an important part of training. You'll run across rugged, hilly terrain. You need strength and endurance to keep going. A cross-country course is much more demanding than running the same distance on a flat track.

In general, you want to run more miles during the off season and early season. This lets you build a conditioning base for endurance. As the season progresses, cut back on your mileage. You want to run enough to stay in top shape but not so much that you can't peak for a competition.

Often, beginning cross-country athletes run about 20 miles a week. That's strictly a guide and your coach can tell you if you should run more or less. As a runner improves, she normally increases her training mileage to a point. Some athletes do as many as 60 miles a week, although that's way too much for many people.

Much of your training, particularly in the off season, will be done alone. But during the season, train with your teammates. The camaraderie will help you maintain your enthusiasm and to keep in mind that cross-country is also a team event. The better you do, the better your team will do.

Warm-ups are as important here as in any track event. You need to break a light sweat and stretch your muscles before running a long distance. Otherwise, you're inviting injury.

This may surprise some people, but cross-country training should also include sprint work, for instance, the 200 meters. Toward the end of a meet, you may be close to the lead. The runner who has the best kick usually will win. If you've worked on sprints during practice, you'll have a big advantage.

Running short distances at high speed also helps build endurance. For instance, your coach might have you run three 200s at full speed with only a minute rest in between. Some coaches like their athletes to run 800 meters several times, with two minutes in between, or a mile with a three-minute rest. It's the same idea.

During training, you'll learn to run when you're tired. At first, you may be tempted to slow down or even stop when you get tired. Successful cross-country runners learn to anticipate fatigue, cope with it, and keep going. Unless you do so, you won't be successful. However, you should never continue to run if you've suffered an injury. You need to be able to tell the difference between soreness and an injury that requires attention.

In cross-country, it's important to develop a sense of pace. On a track, it's easier to keep up with how far you've run. You know the length of each lap. But in cross-country, you're running mile after mile in open areas, and you can lose track of how far you've run and how far you have to go. That's why it's important to check out a course before a competition. They're all different. You can look for markers to help you gauge distances.

The start of a race is extremely important. It's always tempting to run too fast. Your adrenaline is racing. You are among all the other competitors. You think you need to jump out to an early lead, but that's usually a bad idea. Remember, a cross-country race is long. You've got to pace yourself and have enough energy left for a strong finish. No one wins in the first quarter-mile, but you can lose it if you wear yourself out.

In cross-country, no two runners have the same running style. Some have a smooth gait and seem to coast almost effortlessly. Others appear jerky and have a pained expression as if they could collapse at any moment.

You don't win by looking pretty. You win by getting across the finish line first. Still, there are some basic running mechanics that you should learn. They will keep you from wasting motion and putting yourself at a disadvantage.

On flat terrain, you want to run tall, that is, with your body upright and at a slight lean forward. Look straight ahead, not at the ground, to develop a smooth, rhythmic pace. Be careful not to let your head lean backward when you get tired. That's a common problem, and it creates tension in your neck and makes it harder to breath.

Don't overlook your hands and arms. Your fingers should be slightly cupped and remain relaxed. Your arms should pump freely back and forth without extending too far forward or too far to the rear. As a guide, your elbows shouldn't pass your hips going forward, and your hands shouldn't pass your hips going backward. Also, don't let your arms swing past an imaginary vertical line on your chest. If you do, your upper body will likely twist, and you won't maintain a smooth stride.

Stride length is important. There's no need to take long, long strides. In fact, doing so requires too much energy for a distance race. You want a comfortable stride length that you can repeat over and over without straining. You should land on the back part of the ball of your foot, almost flat-footed. Then, your heel will touch down, and you'll push off again with the ball of your foot.

In addition, you don't need to lift your knees high like you would in a sprint. If you keep your knees low, it's easier to maintain a smooth stride.

Hills require special adjustments. Running uphill, lean your entire body slightly into the hill. Don't just bend from the waist. Without leaning, you'll be pulled backward and lose time. Also, take shorter strides, raise your knees a little higher and pump your arms more but still stay under control. These adjustments give you more power to make it up the hill.

Going downhill, you also want to lean forward but not as much. Obviously, if you lean too much, you could fall face first on the ground. However, you don't want to lean backward and run on your heels either. That can be jarring and lead to an uneven pace. As a rule, keep your body perpendicular to the slope. That will let you run under control.

Toward the end of the race, be prepared to sprint if you're battling for the lead. Sprinting form is much different than distance running form. You need to run on your toes, lift your knees high and pump your arms like pistons on a machine. Focus on the finish line and the chance to rest. If you don't make a strong push at the end, you won't get a reward for all the miles you just ran.

MARATHON

The marathon has an almost mystical appeal to many people. The main reason is the sheer distance: 26 miles, 385 yards. To many, that seems like an unbelievable distance to run without stopping. Think of your hometown. Then think of a town about 26 miles away—that's a long way, even by car!

In the past 25 years, marathons have become increasingly popular. Now, it's not uncommon for a friend who doesn't seem particularly athletic to enter and complete a marathon. Part of the reason is better training. Today, there are a slew of books on preparing for a marathon, particularly your first one. They give you a systematic program to follow to help you succeed, including guidance on how far to run early in your training and as race day nears. They also tell you how to care for your body *after* a marathon. Proper recovery is important. You need to restore the fluids your body lost and calories it burned. Otherwise, you can develop cramps and greater soreness.

Running a marathon is like many things in life—preparation is the key. If you start early and train well, you can complete a marathon on your first try. However, there's certainly no shame in not running the whole distance. In fact, many people know they won't. They set a goal of running a certain number of miles in their first marathon, then build on that until they can finish a marathon.

Ideally, you should have some running experience before you decide to undertake a marathon. You need to understand the basics of training and be accustomed to minor aches and pains that accompany running. However, you don't need to be a world-class athlete to set your sights on a marathon. It's important, though, to consult your physician beforehand if you've had any health problems. You don't want to put yourself at risk by running such a long distance.

Some people run one marathon to prove they can do it and have no desire to do it again. Others get hooked on marathons and travel the country competing in them, always trying to lower their time. They may set a goal of competing in the two most famous marathons, the Boston Marathon and New York Marathon. These attract thousands of runners. You've probably seen photos of these marathons—people are shoulder to shoulder for miles. Some people enjoy that atmosphere, others prefer much smaller marathons. No matter where you live, you're likely to find a marathon close by.

As you can imagine, choosing the right shoe is extremely important if you're planning to run for so long. Today's shoes are lighter, more durable, and provide better support than ever. However, there are so many choices that you'll need guidance from a shoe expert. He or she will not only check your shoe size but look at the shape of your foot and your overall build. Heavier people need different shoes than lighter people.

You don't have to buy the most expensive pair, but you don't want to pick a shoe just because it's cheap. If you get an inferior shoe or one that doesn't fit properly, you'll pay for it. You'll be uncomfortable during the race and perhaps develop an injury. Also, you're likely to be sorer after the race.

Picking clothes is not difficult. Stay away from tight, binding outfits. If it's cold, consider a hat and gloves to provide added warmth, but don't overdress. It's wise to wear several layers of light clothing that you can shed along the way if you get too hot.

Always drink enough water, particularly on a hot day. Most marathons have stations with water along the way. Some marathoners like to bring a cheering section of family and friends to give them food and fluids as well as moral support.

SUPERSTAR: JOAN BENOIT SAMUELSON

Joan Benoit Samuelson is a legend in women's marathoning.

In 1984, she won an Olympic gold medal in the event the first time that women had competed in the marathon. Since then, no other American woman has won Olympic gold in the marathon.

Joan recalls being surprised that so many people were watching the 1984 race.

"I thought, this is a morning event. It is the first-ever Olympic Marathon. There aren't going to be a lot of people who care about it," she said. "Was I ever wrong! The number of spectators who lined the course overwhelmed me."

Joan led almost the entire race and entered the stadium for the final leg with a comfortable lead. But she remained nervous.

"When I came into the stadium and saw all the colors and everything, I told myself, 'Listen, just look straight ahead because if you don't, you're probably going to faint."

Joan wasn't expected to win the marathon. The favorite was Grete Waitz of Norway, who had beaten Joan in 10 of 11 races in which they had both competed.

But three miles into the marathon, Joan took the lead and never relinquished it.

"I don't remember much about the actual marathon except running down the Los Angeles freeway all by myself," she said.

It's amazing that she even made it to the Olympics. Seventeen days before the Olympic trials that year, Joan had arthroscopic knee surgery. She feared that she had lost any chance to qualify for the Olympics. For three days after the surgery, she wasn't able to run at all.

Then she began to jog slightly, and her knee felt okay. She added distance. She wasn't sure how she would do, but she entered the Olympic trials and won. Few could believe it. That win gave her a boost of confidence heading into the games.

She followed up her Olympic gold the next year by winning the prestigious Sullivan Award as the country's outstanding amateur athlete. That year, she set an American women's record in the marathon of two hours, 22:21 seconds.

Joan continued to run for more than a decade, but was often slowed by persistent injuries. In 1996, after having two children, she made one final try for the Olympics. Disappointingly, she failed to qualify.

However, she didn't despair. She had been beaten by younger women who had been attracted to the event by her pioneering achievements.

Don't try this . . .

Rosie Ruiz seemed like an unlikely winner of the prestigious Boston Marathon in 1980. Few had heard of the 26-year-old amateur runner, and her victory—as well as record time—immediately raised suspicions.

Turns out, the doubters were right. In one of the most famous hoaxes in sports history, Rosie entered the marathon late—with less than a mile to go—yet claimed to have run the entire 26-mile race and proudly accepted the winner's medal.

However, officials began an extensive review the next day and could find no photos or video of her anywhere along the marathon route. Nor could any other runner recall seeing her except right at the end. A week later, Rosie was stripped of her medal, and it was awarded to Canadian Jacqueline Gareau.

To make the tale more improbable, Rosie never admitted to cheating, even years later. In a 1998 interview, she claimed to have photos and other evidence to prove that she ran the entire marathon. However, she declined to produce the proof.

"It hurts me to know I did something so good but got so many problems," she said in 1998, then 44 years old.

By that time, she had been sued by landlords for nonpayment of rent and been jailed in Miami for selling cocaine to an undercover officer. Yet, she vowed to return to the Boston Marathon and prove that she could run the entire race. She never did.

"What I can promise myself and the American public who believe in me is to run again," said Rosie, a native of Cuba. "I may not win this time, but I will be there and I'll run again, the entire course, just as before."

The actual winner of the 84th Boston Marathon, Jacqueline Gareau, never expressed anger toward Rosie.

"I always took it lightly," she said in an interview in 2000. "In a certain way, I'm better remembered than I would have been if nothing out of the ordinary had happened in that race."

Jacqueline, who was named Canada's top marathoner of the 20th century, was brought back to Boston to receive her medal after the truth came out.

"My only regret is that I missed the euphoria of crossing the finish line and knowing that I had won," she said. "But the people of Boston have more than made that up to me, and I still get so many letters from people who remembered what happened and sort of felt sorry for me."

Completing a marathon is a mental challenge as well as a physical one. Inevitably, you'll become fatigued and tempted to quit. You have to ask yourself if it's worth continuing, particularly if you fear injury. You're not competing in the Olympics, so it's okay, say you've had enough and congratulate yourself on how far you ran.

In marathons, more than in any other competition, you should be competing for fun—for *yourself.* There aren't teams in marathons. It's just you. Marathons let you enjoy healthy competition in which the main opponent is yourself.

TRIATHLON

A marathon used to be the ultimate test of endurance. Today, it's the triathlon. Not only do participants have to run a long distance—sometimes an entire 26-mile marathon—but they also swim and bike on the same day.

Why would anyone want to enter a triathlon? That's a good question. Some people simply like to push their bodies to the limit to see what they can achieve. People may not understand their drive, but triathlon athletes have the same zeal for their event as do marathoners. In fact, some triathletes consider the marathon a mere walk in the park, a tune up for their event.

Triathlons have no set distance. The running, swimming, and bicycling portions can vary widely in length. In recent years, more, shorter triathlons have been held. Few people, after all, have the time to train for an "Ironman" triathlon—one that has a 26-mile run, a 112-mile bike ride, and 2.4-mile swim.

Ironman competitors often train 20 or 30 hours a week or even more. It's hard to have a typical job or family life and be able to devote that much time for training. Today, sprint triathlons are being organized that consist of a five-kilometer run, a 22-kilometer bike ride, and a .75-kilometer swim. You don't have to be a superhuman to complete a triathlon of this distance, although it's certainly a challenge.

The next level up is called the Olympic triathlon. It's made up of a 10-kilometer run, 40-kilometer bike ride, and 1.5-kilometer swim. From there, you have half-Ironman triathlon. As the name implies, it's half the distance of an Ironman, consisting of a 13-mile run, 56-mile bike ride, and 1.2-mile swim.

The half-Ironman is not for the casual weekend athlete. This event takes five or six hours of continuous exertion. Even the shortest triathlons are tough for many people because of the swimming component.

Most of us took swimming lessons as kids, but how many people swim on a regular basis? We're not talking about lying by the pool in the summer. What's more, the swimming part of a triathlon is rarely held in a pool. It's held in the often rough, unpredictable waters of a lake or ocean. It's easy to get disoriented in a large open body of water and begin to panic. Triathlons are closely monitored by officials who watch for signs that a contestant is in trouble.

For many people eyeing their first triathlon, the swimming portion is the scariest part. If your swimming skills aren't up to par, consider taking a refresher course. Local YMCAs, health clubs, and community colleges often offer swimming lessons for people of all ages and abilities. Don't be embarrassed to take a beginner's class if you need one. Also, don't be tempted to simply get a few pointers from a friend. No, you need a series of lessons from an experienced swim instructor to become competent.

Get comfortable swimming in a pool, then try a very short swim in open water *with an experienced open-water swimmer. Never, ever* swim in open water by yourself. Some swimming classes are geared specifically to triathletes and offer tips on open-water swimming. You can do it, but you need to be prepared.

Many books have been written in recent years about triathlons and the proper ways to train. Get one if you're set on competing. These books will give you the advantage of learning from other people's mistakes. Especially when you're young, it's tempting to think that you don't have to read the "instructions" before trying something. Here's an exception. You don't want to exert your body to the point of danger even if you think you're in great shape.

Triathlons attract a variety of men and women, from teens to senior citizens. Lance Armstrong, the four-time winner of the Tour de France bike race, excelled in triathlons as a youngster in Texas. He found that triathlons provided an excellent training ground for cycling, his true love.

Consult your track coach before considering a triathlon. It's unfair to your coach and your teammates to wear yourself out in a triathlon if you're being counted on for the track team. Many triathlons are held in the summer, and that might be a time to try one. But first, think long and hard about whether you have the ability. You may be a great distance runner. But cycling and swimming are different skills altogether. Not everyone who is a good runner is a good cyclist or swimmer. Likewise, skilled cyclist or swimmer can't necessarily run long distances.

Therein lies the challenge and appeal of triathlons: tackling the three diverse components. Our purpose here isn't to prepare you for a triathlon. It's just to point out the demands of the sport and encourage you to build the proper foundation before ever attempting one.

A Boost in the Beginning . . .

In the early 1980s, triathlons were just gaining popularity. The first ones primarily attracted men.

Women's involvement got a big boost by the performance of Julie Moss, a college student, at the 1982 Ironman Triathlon in Hawaii. A former lifeguard, Julie had a big lead near the end of the triathlon and appeared headed for victory.

But with only 20 yards to go, she grew faint and began to wobble. Her weary legs finally gave way, and she collapsed to the pavement. She tried but could not get up. Instead of quitting, she crawled to the finish line as a captivated national TV audience watched. She finished second.

Instantly, the triathlon gained credibility by Julie's courageous performance. Although she didn't win, Julie became more famous than the winner, Kathleen McCartney. More importantly, she ushered in a new age for the triathlon.

"It was a courage thing," one competitor said of Julie's performance. "She was young. She was innocent—therein lies the heroic deed."

MENTAL
PREPARATION
AND NUTRITION

MENTAL PREPARATION

Up to this point, we've discussed the physical training that goes into becoming a top track and field athlete.

But there's another part of training that's sometimes overlooked—the mental side. Today, world-class athletes understand the importance of being mentally prepared to compete. They learn to ignore distractions and setbacks during competition so they can focus all their energies on performing their best.

Years ago, few athletes or coaches talked about psychological preparation. Today they do. Research has clearly shown that the proper mindset can greatly improve the chances of winning. Many athletes use visualization techniques before a meet. That is, they try to imagine the situations they'll encounter during a race—and how they would react. It's almost as if they're watching a movie in their mind to prepare for their performance.

Many athletes believe that visualizing the race beforehand, including imaging potential mistakes, gives them an advantage when the race begins. To some degree, they feel as if they've already run the race. Visualization, then, can ease anxiety and boost confidence.

Visualization also includes recalling a particularly good or bad performance. If you did well, for instance, remember how the race unfolded and how you responded to challenges. Remember how it felt to be in the zone, (in the mindset of the race) with everything working.

On the other hand, it can be useful, although painful, to recall one a dark moment of defeat. Maybe you had a physical breakdown, perhaps a mental breakdown. In either case, you didn't perform up to your capability. You can be determined not to let that happen again.

Coaches sometimes say an athlete is mentally tough. That means he or she has learned to handle an unfortunate occurrence or defeat without cracking. Some athletes are extraordinary talented and well prepared, but a mistake during competition or an unexpected move by an opponent can destroy their confidence and focus. As a result, victory eludes them.

The world of track and field is full of great athletes who never made it to the top. Often, they weren't mentally strong. Today, mental preparation is widely appreciated, and scores of books have been written on the topic. If you're serious about reaching your potential, you should learn more about the psychology of peak performance.

Many athletes do well when the stakes aren't high. But put them in a championship meet with thousands of spectators, and they begin to doubt themselves and tighten up. Mental conditioning includes learning how to excel under pressure. It helps you gear up for competition, while at the same time staying loose. Top Olympians, for instance, often turn in their greatest performances in clutch situations. They win a gold medal and perhaps set a new record against the best athletes in the world.

Naturally, mental preparation must go hand in hand with physical preparation. If you're out of shape and have poor technique, the best mental approach in the world isn't going to help you to win. Take care of the physical part first, then concentrate on the mental side.

In track, as in any sport, you must learn to handle fatigue. It can be your greatest opponent. During a long race, in particular, fatigue inevitably sets in. Mental preparation can help you anticipate fatigue, cope with it and continue to perform at a high level. Some athletes, at the first sign of tiredness, lose their competitive edge. That's what you want to avoid and you can with mental conditioning.

Pushing through fatigue is far different than competing if you're seriously injured. Every athlete, from time to time, has to bow out of a race because of injury. Don't ignore your body's warnings signs, or an injury can become serious and knock you out of competition.

During an event, always stay alert. Watch your opponents and adjust your strategy accordingly. Let your mind tell you how much effort to expend at different times. Learn to control unwise competitive instincts.

Here's an example. Say you're running a middle-distance race against a crosstown rival, and she bursts off the starting line. It's tempting to try to catch her, even if you'll use up too much energy. In this case, you need the mental strength to override your impulse to catch her. By doing so, you've probably increased your chances of winning.

It's common for athletes to try to "psych out" their opponents. For example, they might make an early charge to plant doubt in a rival's mind. Or they might hang back during a race to make an opponent become overconfident then blow past them at the end. Mental preparation includes knowing your opponents' tricks and not falling for them.

In some meets, you may find yourself running all alone. Perhaps you've taken a big lead; perhaps you've fallen way behind. Both situations present mental challenges. If you have a lead, it's tempting to relax, thinking you've already won, or tense up, constantly looking over your shoulder. Either way, you've lost your focus.

On the other extreme, you may be running in a tightly bunched group. Here, too, you must keep your composure. Be alert so you don't trip or get boxed in. Make sure you maintain proper form and pace, despite the distractions.

Many athletes develop a precise routine before competition as a way of staying mentally sharp. For instance, they might do the same stretches or drills in the same order every time. They find that the familiarity of a routine eases their mind and relieves prerace jitters. In a similar way, some athletes like to be alone before competition to improve their focus. Others prefer to joke with teammates as a way of staying loose. Find a routine that works for you and stick with it.

A final word about the mental side. Winning is the goal, but you can have a good competition without coming in first. For instance, maybe you dramatically improved your speed or distance from the last meet. Even though you didn't win, you can gain confidence from your performance. That confidence can make you mentally stronger next time, when you may win.

See each performance as a building block. Don't obsess on what you didn't do right. Focus on what you accomplished. That's the way to keep improving.

NUTRITION

Just as mental preparation is sometimes overlooked in training, so is nutrition. Young athletes often think they can eat anything without hurting their performance. Coaches, too, are guilty of not stressing the importance of diet.

Athletes need to learn the basics of nutrition and how to develop healthy eating habits. We're not talking about getting on an impossibly strict diet. Nor are we talking about taking expensive food supplements that may be useless or, worse, harmful.

We're talking about using common sense when you eat. Don't load up on greasy, spicy food the night before a meet. In fact, limit that kind of food all the time. It's okay to enjoy guilty food every now and then, but don't live on a diet of ice cream and candy bars.

Learn about the basic components of food—protein, carbohydrates and fats—and figure out a reasonable caloric intake for each day. There are countless books on nutrition in any bookstore or library. They discuss, for instance, which foods are high in carbohydrates, protein, and fat.

There's both consensus and disagreement on what constitutes a proper diet. Many top athletes focus on carbohydrates, which are found in starchy foods such as potatoes, bread, and pasta. Carbohydrates are an excellent energy source. Distance athletes, for instance, often have a diet in which 70 percent of the calories come from carbohydrates. Some even increase their carbohydrate intake several days before a competition. This is known as carbo-loading, but is not as popular now as it was in the past. New research is mixed on whether carbo-loading boosts performance.

However, it's always a good idea to eat a sound meal two to four hours before competition. Pick light foods and keep the serving sizes reasonable. Bread and fruit are good choices. Again, use common sense. No super-sized burritos with chili and cheese a half-hour before a meet.

Because young people often have a high metabolism, they don't have to count calories as carefully as their elders. In fact, many young athletes probably have no idea how many calories they take in a day. That's okay as long as they're eating right and keeping their weight under control.

If their eating habits are good, there's probably no need to take vitamins or minerals, many nutrition experts say. They say a balanced diet provides all the vitamins and minerals that most people need.

Unfortunately, some young athletes, particularly girls, develop eating disorders. These can be extremely serious, even life-threatening. No doubt you've heard of anorexia and bulimia. Anorexia is when people starve themselves. Bulimia is when people eat and then throw up to keep from gaining weight. Eating disorders stem from a false body image and a compulsive need to get thinner. People suffering from eating disorders consider themselves overweight, even though it's obvious to others that they are dangerously thin.

Sometimes parents and coaches inadvertently make a young athlete overly conscious of her weight. This can create the potential for an eating disorder. Even a well-meaning suggestion that a young athlete could improve her time by losing a few pounds can have a devastating psychological effect on some girls. No athletic accomplishment is worth the risk of developing an eating disorder. Parents and coaches should be acutely aware of warning signs.

For instance, does a girl seem to be skipping meals? Has she had a sudden weight loss? Is she defensive about her weight? Do you suspect she might be taking laxatives or diet pills to lose weight? Few people readily acknowledge an eating problem, and it's a difficult subject to approach. Ask a doctor or counselor about the best way to proceed if you have concerns about someone.

We've discussed food, but let's not forget liquids. You may have heard this over and over, but it bears repeating: Drink plenty of water! This is good advice for a person who sits a desk all day. And it's particularly good advice for someone undergoing strenuous workouts.

Don't just drink when you're thirsty. Drink before you get thirsty to stay properly hydrated. If you don't, you'll tire more easily. Worse, you could become dehydrated or even suffer heat stroke. These are serious conditions that include cramps, dizziness and nausea.

Years ago, some coaches withheld water from athletes during practice, thinking they were making them tough. Today, we know that's nonsense and it is dangerous. Drink plenty of water before, during, and after a workout. Most of the popular sports drinks are okay but not absolutely necessary. Water does a good job of replenishing your body.

Finally, let's say a word about performance-enhancing drugs. Much has been written about the dangers of steroids. Athletes in all sports, including track and field, have abused steroids and other drugs to build muscle and try to improve their performance. Sometimes, they've been successful in the short term. You may have heard of Ben Johnson, a Canadian sprinter who had a remarkable performance in the 1988 Olympics. He won the gold medal in the 100 meters and set a world record 9.79 seconds or so it seemed.

Later, tests showed that he had used anabolic steroids, and he was stripped of his medals. Five years later, he was banned for life from track and field because he tested positive again for drugs.

In short, it's a huge mistake to consider taking steroids or any other performance drug. First, they're illegal, and you can be banned from competition for using them. Second, they can permanently damage your body. Steroids have been associated with heart attacks, strokes, blood clots, and liver cancer, according to the National Institute on Drug Abuse. Among females, they can disrupt the normal hormone balance, reduce breast size, increase body hair, and make the skin coarse.

Stay away from performance-enhancing drugs. They're trouble.

Eat right, drink plenty of fluids, and train hard. That's the foundation of success in track and field.

10
STRETCHES AND WEIGHT LIFTING

Track and field events place great demands on the body, even young ones. Athletes who fail to properly warm up won't perform as well as they could and might suffer a season-ending injury.

STRETCHING

Proper stretching involves multiple parts of your body. For instance, athletes in the running events don't just stretch their legs, and those in the throwing events don't just stretch their arms and chest.

A top performance in any event calls upon the muscles in your entire body so it makes sense to have a comprehensive stretching routine. We've listed some basic stretches here that cover the main muscles groups you would use in any event. There are certainly other stretches you could do in addition to or in place of these. Your coach may also have some favorites.

Our point is to emphasize the importance of making stretching a regular part of your workout. Whichever exercises you choose, stretching should always be done gradually and gently with no sudden movements or bouncing. These can cause injury. Stay relaxed during stretching. You'll get the most benefit, and you'll prepare yourself mentally for competing.

TYPES OF STRETCHES

Hurdler's Stretch

Sit on the floor with your left leg straight in front of you. Bend your right leg so that your right foot rests against your groin

Hurdler's stretch

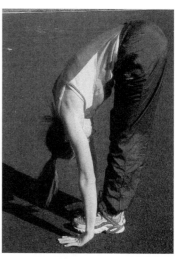

Palms on ground

and inside left thigh. Lean forward with your left arm and grab the toes of your left foot. Gradually pull your foot toward your chest. Repeat with right leg extended.

Palms on Ground

Stand with your feet together. Bend from the waist and lower your upper body until your head is near your shins. Gradually place palms on the ground in front of you. Hold.

Leg extension

Leg Extensions

Lie on your back. Straighten your right leg and extend it toward the sky. Grab the back of your right leg and slowly pull it toward your chest. Point toes down toward your face for maximum effect. Repeat with left leg.

Ankle pull

Groin stretch

Ankle Pull

Lie on your stomach. Bend your right leg at the knee so your heel approaches your buttocks. Grab your ankle and gradually press your leg down. Repeat with left leg.

Groin Stretch

Sit on the floor with your legs bent and feet pulled against your groin. Your kneecaps point to the side, and the bottoms of your feet touch. Grab the outside of your ankles and slowly press your thighs toward the floor.

Torso Bend

Stand with your legs together, hands on your hips and elbows out to the side. Cross your right foot in front of your left. (Legs will touch.) Bend from the waist, lowering your head toward your knees. Hold, then gradually rise up. Repeat with left foot in front.

Leg Crossover

Lie on your back with your legs extended straight in front and arms pointing to the side at 90 degrees. Raise your right leg so that it's pointing at the sky. Slowly lower your right leg across your body until your foot touches your left hand. Hold. Then repeat with left leg.

Body Lean

Sit on the floor with your legs extended and angled in a V. Raise your right arm, bend it at the elbow and place your forearm on the top of

Torso bend (above and right)

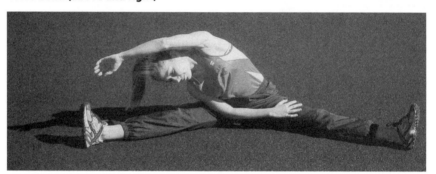

Body lean

Torso twist

Leg crossover

your head. Lean your upper body to the left as far as possible. Repeat with left forearm on top of head, leaning to the right.

Torso Twist

Sit with your hands behind your hips and legs extended in front. Bend your left leg and place your left foot across your right knee. Hold it there and slowly twist your upper body to the left. Then do the reverse. Place your right foot across your left knee and twist your upper body to the right.

Back Roll

Lie on your back and bend your knees toward your chest. Grab the underside of your thighs and pull them down until your hips rise slightly off floor. Hold.

Neck Roll

Lie on your back. Bend your knees and lower your legs to your chest, with your feet facing the sky. Grab the lower part of your back near your buttocks, then hold this position. Avoid placing too much pressure on neck.

Back roll

WEIGHT LIFTING

Years ago, coaches didn't recommend weight training for track and field athletes, especially sprinters. They thought that weight lifting would make athletes bulky and stiff, qualities you certainly didn't want to run fast, jump high, or throw far.

Neck roll

Today, however, coaches know that weight training done properly is a tremendous aid. Increased strength can lead to better results in any event and help prevent injury. Weight lifting is more often associated with boys, but girls can benefit just as much. And you won't end up looking like a body builder.

It's important to select the right weight lifting exercises for maximum results. Here, we group several common, effective exercises into two categories those for upper body and those for lower body. For some, you use barbells. For other, you use weight machines commonly found in gyms. Just as we said about stretches, there are many other good weight lifting exercises you can choose.

Always be careful when lifting weights. Proper form is extremely important. Improper form can lead to serious injury. Lifting weights incorrectly is worse than not lifting at all.

Here are a few general guidelines for correct weight lifting:

- Stretch before each workout.
- Lift in a smooth and controlled manner—no jerking.
- Don't strain.
- Never hold your breath. Inhale as you lower the weight, exhale as you lift.
- While you're a beginner, never work out alone. Have a coach or experienced weight lifter to guide you and assist if you try to lift too much.
- Rarely try to lift your maximum weight. This can easily produce injuries and isn't as beneficial as numerous repetitions at a lower weight. Early in the off-season, do fewer repetitions and more sets. For instance, you might do two sets of 15 repetitions (reps). As the season approaches, you would do three sets of 12 reps. During the season, you might do four sets of eight reps.
- Add weight gradually to the barbell as you build strength. For instance, don't suddenly increase your training weight in an exercise by 20 or 30 pounds.
- Keep weight lifting sessions relatively short—less than an hour. Longer sessions can become tedious and lead to sloppy form and overexertion.
- Change your weight lifting exercises every four to six weeks to avoid monotony and to work new muscles.
- Don't work out the same muscles two days in a row. For instance, train your lower body on Monday, Wednesday, and Friday and upper body on Tuesday and Thursday. Or, you can work out your whole body on one day and then skip a day before working out again.
- Keep a written record of your workouts, including the weight you used and number of repetitions.

LOWER BODY

Leg Extension

This is done on a leg machine. You sit on the end of a bench and dangle your legs toward the floor. There's a bar that rests against the front of your shins. Gradually push up on the bar. A cable connected to the bar raises a stack of weights for resistance. Lower and repeat. Make sure not to use too much weight at first.

Leg Curl

This is done on a machine. Lie on a bench on your stomach. A bar rests against your Achilles tendons. Bend your knees to raise the bar toward your buttocks. A stack of weights is also used on this machine.

Leg Press

This is done on a machine. Sit with your knees bent toward you and feet resting on pedals. Push against the pedals, raising a stack of weights until your legs straighten.

Squat

This is done with a barbell that starts out on a rack about shoulder height. To perform this exercise, back up to the bar. Bend your knees slightly and grab the barbell off the rack behind your head. Rest it on your shoulders until it feels comfortable. Now, bend your knees and lower your torso until your thighs are parallel to the floor. Then raise up.

Calf Raise

This is also done with a barbell resting on a rack. Once you place the barbell on your shoulders (as described above), place the front of your foot on a board or other stable object about two inches high. Now raise up on your feet as high as possible—your heels will be several inches off the ground.

UPPER BODY

Bench Press

This is done with a barbell or machine. Lie on a bench with a barbell or machine handle just above your chest. Place your hands shoulder-width on the bar and press straight up until your elbows lock. Lower gradually.

Shoulder Press

This is done with a barbell or a machine, while standing. Place your hands shoulder-width on a barbell or machine handle in front of your chest. Lift straight up overhead until your elbows lock. Lower slowly.

Upright Rowing

Use a barbell. Grab it with your hands toward the middle, about six inches apart. Start with the bar in front of your thighs. Lift the bar smoothly until your hands reach your chin. Lower the bar gradually until it's in front of your thighs again.

Lat Pull-Downs

This is done on a machine. Grab a long horizontal bar that's overhead and has ends that angle toward the floor. Hold the bar at both ends, then pull it down in front of your chest until it reaches your waist. Let the bar rise back up until the weight stack comes to a stop.

Dips

No weights are used for this exercise. Find a set of dip bars—horizontal, parallel bars that are shoulder-width and chest high. Place your palms on top the bars. (You may need a stool to get high enough to do so.) Press down with your hands and lift your body until your elbows lock. Then bend your elbows and gradually lower your body until your chest reaches the bars.

Biceps Curls

This is done with a barbell. Place your hands under the bar with palms facing up, about shoulder width. Start with the bar in front of your thighs. Bend your elbows and raise the bar until it reaches your chest. (The range of motion resembles an arc.) Then lower the bar to your thighs.

Triceps Pull-Downs

This is done with a machine. Grab the same long horizontal bar (described above) that's used for lat pull-downs. Place your hands on top the bar and close to the middle, about six inches apart. Start with the bar in front of your chest. Push down until the bar reaches your waist. (The range of motion resembles an arc.) Let the bar rise back up until the weight stack comes to a stop.

Crunches

Lie on the floor with your legs bent halfway and knees facing the sky. Cross your arms on top your chest. Bend at the waist and raise your upper body about six inches off the floor, rolling your shoulders in slightly. Lower your body to the floor.

ASSOCIATIONS AND WEBSITES

Amateur Athletic Union
P.O. Box 22409
Lake Buena Vista, FL 32830
http://www.aausports.org

American Running
4405 East West Highway
Suite 405
Bethesda, MD 20814
http://www.americanrunning.org

National Federation of State Highway Associations
P.O. Box 690
Indianapolis, IN 46206
http://www.nfhs.org

National Youth Sports Safety Foundation
One Beacon Street
Suite 3333
Boston, MA 02108
http://www.nyssf.org

USA Track & Field
One RCA Dome
Suite 140
Indianapolis, IN 46225
http://www.usatf.org

Women's Sports Foundation
Eisenhower Park
East Meadow, NY 11554
http://www.womenssportsfoundation.org

FURTHER READING

Alter, Michael J. *Sport Stretch.* Champaign, Illinois: Human Kinetics, 1998, 1990.

Bowerman, William J., and Freeman, William H. *High Performance Training for Track and Field.* Champaign, Illinois: Leisure Press, 1991.

Carr, Gerry. *Fundamentals of Track and Field.* Champaign, Illinois: Human Kinetics, 1999, 1991.

Fortin, Francois. *Sports: The Complete Visual Reference.* Buffalo, New York: Firefly Books, 2000.

Greene, Larry, and Pate, Russ. *Training for Young Distance Runners.* Champaign, Illinois: Human Kinetics, 1995.

Jacoby, Ed, and Fraley, Bob. *Complete Book of Jumps.* Champaign, Illinois: Human Kinetics, 1995.

Micheli, Lyle J., M.D., with Mark Jenkins. *Sports Medicine Bible for Young Athletes.* Naperville, Illinois: Sourcebooks Inc., 2001.

Rogers, Joseph L. *USA Track & Field Coaching Manual.* Champaign, Illinois: Human Kinetics, 2000.

Wallace, Edward L., Jr. *Track & Field Coach's Survival Guide.* Paramus, New Jersey: Parker Publishing Company, 1998.

INDEX

Boldface page numbers denote major treatment of a topic. Those in *italics* denote illustrations.

4 x 100 relay race
  exchange zone in 58–59
  lanes in 59
  records in 65
  responsibility of each runner in 63
  sample workout for 70–73
4 x 400 relay race 62
  exchange zone in 59
  lanes in 59
  records in 65
  responsibility of each runner in 64
  sample workout for 73–75
4 x 800 relay race 65
100-meter hurdles 28
  introduction as women's Olympic event 29

placement of hurdles in 29, 32–33
records in 33
sample workout for 39–42
100-meter race
  lanes in 7
  records in 13
  sample workouts for 20–22
  starting blocks in 7
200-meter race
  in heptathlon 148
  introduction as women's Olympic event 7
  lanes in 7
  records in 13
  sample workouts for 20–22
  starting blocks in 7
  turns in 11–12
300-meter hurdles 28, 32–33
400-meter hurdles 28
  introduction as women's Olympic event 29

placement of hurdles in 29, 32–33
records in 33
sample workout for 42–44
400-meter race 5
  introduction as women's Olympic event 7
  lanes in 7
  records in 14
  sample workouts for 22–24
  starting blocks in 7, 10
  turns in 11–12
800-meter race 45–46
  in heptathlon 148
  introduction as women's Olympic event 46
  records in 48–49
  sample workout for 52–54
1,500-meter race 45–46
  introduction as women's Olympic event 46

records in 49
sample workout
for 52–54
3,000-meter race
45–46, 46
records in 49
sample workout
for 52–54

A

Abney, Tiffany 65
acceleration
drills for 17, 69
in sprints 11–12,
14
acceleration drill
69
add-ons drill 38
adhesive tape 110
airborne action
long jump 91, 91,
92, 93
triple jump 102,
103
Alexis, Joyce 13
Amateur Athletic
Union 174
American Running
174
anchor 63, 64
ankle pull stretch
167, 167
anorexia 163–164
approach
high jump 78–81,
79, 80
javelin 138–140,
139
long jump 90
pole vault 112,
112
triple jump 99,
100
approach practice
drill 86

arm movement
cross-country
152–153
hurdles 31
middle-/long-
distance races 47
sprints 10
Armstrong, Lance 158
arm swing drill 135
Ashford, Evelyn 35
Associated Press
Female Athlete of
the Year Award 19
associations 174
athletic belts 122

B

back pushes drill 117
back roll stretch
170, 170
backward handstand
drill 116
Bailey, Julene 115
bamboo poles 110
bar
high jump 78, 82,
82–84
pole vault 110,
114, 114–115,
115–116
basketball throw drill
142, 142
basketball throws
against a wall drill
127
basketball throws for
distance drill 128
baton 58
baton exchange
4 x 400 meter
relay race 62
difficulty of 57–58
downsweep
method 61,
61–62, 62

faults and fixes for
66–67
upsweep method
59–61, 60
Batten, Kim 33, **44**
Beamon, Bob 89
beginning jumping
drill 85
Bell, Jill 93
bench press weight
training exercise
172
biceps curls weight
training exercise
173
body lean stretch
167, 168, 169
Boston Marathon
154, 156
bottle drill 67
bounce drill 67
bounding 17, 18
bounding drill 85,
105, 105
"boxed in" 45, 50
box jumping drill
106
box stepping drill
105–106
Boyle, Dana 49
Boyle, Elizabeth 115
Bradley, Tiffany 65
Broussard, Alicia
104
Budd, Zola **55–56**
bulimia 163–164
"bunched" starting
position 7, 8
Butler, Julie 141

C

calf raise weight
training exercise
172

caloric intake 163
carbohydrates 163
carbo-loading 163
Carter, Michael 126
Carter, Michelle
    125, **126**
Caruthers, Regina
    65
chalk drill 37
Chistyakova, Galina
    93
Clark-Diggs, Joetta
    54
clearing the bar
    high jump 82, *82*
    pole vault *114*,
        114–115,
        115–116
cleats
    for hurdling 29
    for sprints 7
Clinton, Bill 20
clothes (for marathon
    running) 154
complete throw with
    rubber ring drill
    135
consistency drills
    17–18
Coubertin, Pierre de
    1
Cross, Brandi 14
cross-country 146,
    150–153
cross-country train-
    ing drill 51
crunches weight
    training exercise
    173
cycling 157–158

D

Darden, Dominique
    65
Davis, Jessica 65

Debartolo, Elizabeth
    134
Decker, Mary 3,
    55–56
delays (before events)
    48
Delemen, Keyotta
    65
Devers, Gail 4, 29,
    40, 41, 69
Didrikson, Babe 2
diet 162–164
dips weight training
    exercise 173
discus (equipment)
    130
discus (event)
    130–136
    basics of 130–131
    drills for 135–136
    faults and fixes for
        134–135
    grip in 131
    records in 134
    safety concerns
        with 131
    sample workouts
        for 136
    techniques for
        131–133,
        131–134
disqualification
    high jump 78
    hurdles 29–30, 33
    pole vault 109
    relay races 58
    sprints 7
Donkova, Yordanka
    33
double-arm tech-
    nique 101
downsweep (baton
    exchange method)
    61, 61–62, *62*
Dragila, Stacy 3,
    115, **119**

Dressel, Lisa 49
drills
    for acceleration
        17
    acceleration drill
        69
    add-ons drill 38
    approach practice
        drill 86
    arm swing drill
        135
    back pushes drill
        117
    backward hand-
        stand drill 116
    basketball throw
        drill 142, *142*
    basketball throws
        against a wall
        drill 127
    basketball throws
        for distance drill
        128
    beginning jumping
        drill 85
    bottle drill 67
    bounce drill 67
    bounding drill 85,
        105, *105*
    box jumping drill
        106
    box stepping drill
        105–106
    chalk drill 37
    complete throw
        with rubber ring
        drill 135
    consistency drills
        17–18
    cross-country
        training drill
        51
    discus 135–136
    for endurance 17
    figure eight drill
        85, 86

five-step throw with javelin drill 144

flexibility drills 15, 17

four-step throw drill 142, *143*

gliding practice drill 129

high jump 84–86, *84–86*

high-stepping drill 35, *36*, 85

hit the spot drill 69

hopping drill 15, *16*, 17

hurdle hops drill 51, *52*, *106*, 106–107

hurdles 35–38, *36–38*

interval sprints drill 51

javelin 142–144, *142–144*

jogging drill 35

jogging handoff drill *68*, 68–69

jumping rope drill 95

leading leg drill 37, *37*

long jump 94–96, *95*, *96*

lunges drill 15, *16*, 94, *95*

middle-/long-distance races 51–52

for muscle tone 15, *16*, 17, *18*

one-legged hurdle hops drill 84, *84*

pace practice drill 51

pole vault 116–117

pyramid sprints drill 51

relay races 67–68, *68*

rope climb drill 116

rope swing drill 116

run-ups drill 94

shot put *127*, 127–129, *128*

shot put from standing position drill 128

simple lift drill 127, *127*

single-leg dips drill 84–85, *85*

single-leg hops drill 95

sitting throw drill 135

spin practice drill 135

sprints 15–20, *16*, *18*

stair hop drill 38

standing handoff drill 67

standing long jump drill 95, *96*

standing throw with a javelin drill 143, *143*, *144*

starting position drills 15

step and sling drill 135

step and throw drill 142

step-ups drill 95, *96*

for stride length 17–18

swing and rotate drill 116–117

time travel drill 51

trailing leg drill 37, *38*

triple jump *105*, 105–106, *106*

underwater running drill 52

uphill run drill 38

uphill runs drill 51

wall exercise drill 35, *36*

wrist flips drill 127, *128*

Duhart, Nicole 104

Dula, Noel 65

Dwyer, Evelyn 65

E

East Germany 65

eating disorders 163–164

Edmonson, E. 65

Edmonson, Malika 65

elimination. *See* disqualification

"elongated" starting position 7, *9*

Emanuel, A. 65

endurance drills 17

exchange zone 58–59

4 x 100 relay race 58–59

4 x 400 relay race 59

F

false starts 7
fatigue 152, 161
fats 163
faults and fixes
    discus 134–135
    high jump 83–84
    hurdles 34–35
    javelin 141–142
    long jump 93–94
    middle-/long-dis-
        tance races
        49–50
    pole vault
        115–116
    relays 66–67
    shot put 125–126
    sprints 14–15
    triple jump 104
Favor, Suzy 49
fiberglass poles 110
figure eight drill 85,
    86
finishing (in sprints)
    12, 12–13
first runner (in 4 x
    100 meter relay
    race) 64
five-step throw with
    javelin drill 144
flexibility drills 15,
    17
"FloJo." *See* Griffith-
    Joyner, Florence
Fosbury, Dick 77, 89
"Fosbury Flop" 77
foul(s)
    discus 131
    javelin 137
    long jump 89, 93
    pole vault 110
    shot put 121
    triple jump 99
four-step throw drill
    142, *143*

fourth runner
    4 x 100 meter
        relay race 63
    4 x 400 meter
        relay race 64
full stride (in sprints)
    12, *12*

G

Gaines, Chryste
    69–70
Gareau, Jacqueline
    156
Giannascoli, Rachel
    65
glide method (shot
    put) 121, 122, *123*
gliding practice drill
    129
Glover, Michelle 13
Grayson, E. 65
Green, Jenny 115
Griffith-Joyner, Flo-
    rence xviii, 13,
    19–20, 75
grip
    discus 131
    javelin 137–138,
        138
    pole vault 110,
        111
    shot put 121
Grizzle, Tamieka 49
groin stretch 167,
    167

H

half-Ironman
    triathlon 157
Hall, M. 65
hang technique *92*,
    93
"heats" 7

Henderson, Monique
    13, 14
Henry, Angela 93
heptathlon 146–148,
    147–150
high jump 76, **77–88**
    basics of 78
    drills for 84–86,
        84–86
    faults and fixes
        83–84
    in heptathlon 148
    records in 83
    sample workout
        for 86–88
    techniques for
        78–82, *79–82*
high-stepping drill
    35, *36*, 85
hills 153
history of track and
    field **1–4**
hitch-kick technique
    91, *91*
hit the spot drill 69
Hopp, Cecilia 49
hop phase (triple
    jump) 99, 100, *100*,
    101, 104
hopping drill 15, *16*,
    17
hurdle hops drill 51,
    52, *106*, 106–107
hurdler's stretch
    165, *166*
hurdles (equipment)
    29
hurdles (event)
    28–44. *See also*
    100-meter hurdles;
    400-meter hurdles
    300-meter hurdles
    28, 32–33
    basics of 29–30
    drills for 35–38,
        36–38

faults and fixes for
34–35
in heptathlon
148
knocking down
hurdles in
29–30
penalties/disquali-
fication in
29–30, 33
records in 33
sample workouts
for 39–44
techniques for *30*,
30–33, *31*
hydration 154, 164

I

injuries 6, 24–26
assessment of 25
early detection of
25
prevention of 25,
122
treatment of 25–26
International Ama-
teur Athlete Feder-
ation 150
International Olym-
pic Committee 2
interval sprints drill
51
"Ironman" triathlon
157, 159

J

javelin (equipment)
137
javelin (event) 120,
137–145
basics of 137
drills for 142–144,
142–144

faults and fixes for
141–142
grip in 137–138,
138
in heptathlon
148
records in 141
safety concerns
with 137
sample workouts
for 144–145
techniques for
137–140,
138–140
Jesse Owens
National Youth
Games 19
jogging drill 35
jogging handoff drill
68, 68–69
Johnson, Ben 164
Johnson, Yolanda 33
Jones, Marion xviii,
26–27, 69
Joyner-Kersee, Jackie
xviii, 4, 147, 148,
150
jumping drills
beginning jumping
drill 85
box jumping drill
106
high jump 84–86,
84–86
jumping rope drill
95
long jump 94–96,
95, 96
standing long
jump drill 95,
96
triple jump *105*,
105–106, *106*
jumping events
76–77. *See also*
high jump; long

jump; pole vault;
triple jump
jumping rope drill 95
jump phase (triple
jump) 99, 102, *103*

K

Kendrick, Essence
65
"kick"
cross-country 151
middle-/long-
distance races
45, 48, 50
Koch, Marita 14
Kostadinova, Stefka
83
Kratochvilova, Jarmil
48
Kravets, Inessa 104

L

landing
high jump 82, *82*
long jump 93
pole vault 114–115
triple jump 102,
103
landing area (in high
jump) 78
lanes
4 x 100 relay race
59
4 x 400 relay race
59
100-meter race 7
200-meter race 7
400-meter race 7
lat pull-downs
weight training
exercise 173
leading leg drill 37,
37

lead runner (in 4 x 100 meter relay race) 63
leaning at finish line (in sprints) 13
leg crossover stretch 167, *169*
leg curl weight training exercise 171–172
leg extensions stretch 166, *166*
leg extension weight training exercise 171
leg press weight training exercise 172
liquids 164
Lisovskaya, Natalya 125
long-distance races. *See* middle-/long-distance races
long jump 76, **88–99**
    basics of 89
    drills for 94–96, *95, 96*
    faults and fixes for 93–94
    in heptathlon 148
    records in 93
    sample workouts for 97–99
    techniques for 90–93, *91, 92*
lunges drill 15, *16, 94, 95*
lunging at finish line (in sprints) 13

M

Malone, Sarah 141
Manning, Domenique 33

marathons 146, **153–157**
McCartney, Kathleen 159
McKinney, Shante 65
"medium" starting position 7, *8*
Menéndez, Osleidys 141
mental preparation **160–162**
Merritt, Shakerrah 65
middle-/long-distance races **45–56**. *See also* 800-meter race; 1,500-meter race; 3,000-meter race
    basics of 46
    drills for 51–52
    faults and fixes for 49–50
    records in 48–49
    sample workouts for 52–54
    techniques for 47–48
Miller, Inger 44, **69–70**
Milliat, Alice 2
Mills, Chrissy 83
Mitchell, Rebecca 49
Moore, LaShauntea 13
Moss, Julie 159
muscle tone drills 15, *16,* 17, *18*

N

National Federation of High School Coaches 150

National Federation of State and High School Associations 3
National Federation of State Highway Associations 174
National Institute on Drug Abuse 164
National Youth Sports Safety Foundation 174
neck roll stretch 170, *170*
Nesbit, Joan 50
New York Marathon 154
Nickoley, Trisha 49
nutrition **162–164**

O

Olympic Games
    Kim Batten in 44
    Bob Beamon in 89
    Zola Budd in 55–56
    Michael Carter in 126
    cross-country 150
    Mary Decker in 55–56
    Gail Devers in 69
    Stacy Dragila in 119
    Dick Fosbury in 77, 89
    Chryste Gaines in 69–70
    Florence Griffith-Joyner in 19
    heptathlon 148
    high jump 78
    history of 1–2
    hurdles 29

Marion Jones in
xviii, 26, 27, 69
Jackie Joyner-
Kersee in xviii,
147
long jump 89
middle-/long-
distance races
in 46
Inger Miller in
69–70
pole vault 109
Joan Benoit Sam-
uelson in 155
sprints 7
triathlon in 157
triple jump 99
women in 3–4
Women's
Olympics 2
Olympic triathlon
157
one-legged hurdle
hops drill 84, *84*
"on your marks"
position 9, *10*, 15
open-water swim-
ming 158

P

pace
cross-country 152
middle-/long-
distance races
46
pace practice drill 51
palms on ground
stretch 166
Payne, Roshanna 65
penalties (in hurdles)
29–30
performance-enhanc-
ing drugs 164
Pickler, Diana
149–150

Pickler, Julie
149–150
Plasticine 89
pole carry 110, 111,
111, 112
pole plant 112–113,
113
poles 109–110
pole vault 3, 76–77,
109–119
basics of 109–110
drills for 116–117
faults and fixes for
115–116
grip in 110, 111
records in 115
sample workouts
for 117–119
techniques for
110–115,
111–114
Powell, Suzy 134
Powell, Virginia Gin-
nie 33
preparation for
marathons
153–154
problems. *See* faults
and fixes
protein 163
"psyching out" oppo-
nents 162
pyramid sprints drill
51

Q

Qu Yunxia 49

R

Ratcliff, C. 65
Ray, Susie 125
Reinsch, Gabriele
134

relays **57–75**. *See
also* 4 x 100 relay
race; 4 x 400 relay
race
4 x 800 relay race
65
basics of 58–59
drills for 67–68,
68
faults and fixes for
66–67
records in 64–65
responsibilities of
runners in 63–64
sample workouts
for 70–75
techniques for
59–62, *60–62*
release
discus 132,
134–135
javelin 140, *140*,
141, 142
Rice, Grantland 2
ring
discus 130
shot put 121
Rogers, Danielle 65
rope climb drill 116
rope swing drill 116
rosin 110
Ross, Tiffany 33
routine 162
rubber ring drill 135
Rudolph, Wilma
2–3, 26, 67
Ruiz, Rosie 156
running races. *See
specific type of
race, e.g.:* sprints
running style 152
run-up area 78
run-ups drill 94
runway
javelin 137
long jump 89

S

safety
  discus 131
  javelin 137
  swimming 158
sail technique *92,
  93, 103*
sample workouts
  4 x 100 relay race
    70–73
  4 x 400 relay race
    73–75
  100-meter hurdles
    39–42
  100-meter race
    20–22
  200-meter race
    20–22
  400-meter hurdles
    42–44
  400-meter race
    22–24
  800-meter race
    52–54
  1,500-meter race
    52–54
  discus 136
  high jump 86–88
  hurdles 39–44
  javelin 144–145
  long jump 97–99
  middle-/long-
    distance races
    52–54
  pole vault
    117–119
  relays 70–75
  shot put 129–130
  sprints 20–24
  triple jump
    107–109
Samuelson, Joan
  Benoit **155**
sand pit 89
Saulsberry, Kamia 65

second runner
  4 x 100 meter
    relay race 63
  4 x 400 meter
    relay race 64
"set" position 9–10,
  11, 14, 15
set-up (for discus)
  131–132, *132, 133*
shoes
  for high jumping
    78
  for hurdling 29
  for marathon run-
    ning 154
  for sprints 7
shot put (equipment)
  121
shot put (event)
  121–130
  basics of 121–122
  drills for *127,*
    127–129, *128*
  faults and fixes for
    125–126
  grip in 121
  in heptathlon
    148
  Jackie Joyner-
    Kersee's best dis-
    tances in 147
  records in 125
  sample workouts
    for 129–130
  techniques for
    122–125, *123,
    124*
shot put from stand-
  ing position drill
  128
shoulder press
  weight training
  exercise 172
Simons, Deana 104
simple lift drill 127,
  127

Sims, Adrianne 83
single-leg dips drill
  84–85, *85*
single-leg hops drill
  95
sitting throw drill
  135
Smith, Christina 65
Smith, Stephanie 14
Solomon, Shalonda
  65
Soviet Union 65
spin method (shot
  put) 121, 122–125,
  124
spin practice drill
  135
sprints **5–27**. *See
  also* 100-meter
  race; 200-meter
  race; 400-meter
  race
  acceleration in
    11–12
  basics of 6–7
  drills for 15–20,
    16, 18
  faults and fixes for
    14–15
  injuries related to
    24–26
  records in 13–14
  sample workouts
    for 20–24
  starting tech-
    niques 7–11
  techniques for
    7–13, *8–11*
squat weight training
  exercise 172
stair hop drill 38
standards 110
standing handoff drill
  67
standing long jump
  drill 95, *96*

standing throw with
  a javelin drill 143,
  143, 144
starting blocks 6–7
  100-meter race 7
  200-meter race 7
  400-meter race 7,
    10
starting position
  drills 15
step and sling drill
  135
step and throw drill
  142
step phase (triple
  jump) 99, 101, *102,*
  104
step-ups drill 95, *96*
steroids 164
Stewart, Talia 33
stopboard
  javelin 137
  shot put 121
strategy 45–46, 48,
  161
stretches/stretching
  6, **165–170,**
  166–170
  ankle pull stretch
    167, *167*
  back roll stretch
    170, *170*
  body lean stretch
    167, *168,* 169
  groin stretch 167,
    167
  hurdler's stretch
    165, *166*
  leg crossover
    stretch 167,
    169
  leg extensions
    stretch 166,
    166
  neck roll stretch
    170, *170*

palms on ground
  stretch 166
torso bend stretch
  167, *168*
torso twist stretch
  168, 169
stride length
  cross-country
    153
  drills for 17–18
  middle-/long-
    distance races
    47
  sprints 13
success stories
  Michelle Carter
    126
  Diana Pickler
    149–150
  Julie Pickler
    149–150
Sullivan Award 19,
  155
superstars
  Kim Batten **44**
  Zola Budd **55–56**
  Mary Decker
    55–56
  Gail Devers **40,**
    41, 69
  Stacy Dragila **119**
  Chryste Gaines
    69–70
  Florence Griffith-
    Joyner **19–20**
  Marion Jones
    26–27, 69
  Inger Miller
    69–70
  Joan Benoit
    Samuelson **155**
Swain, Treani 49,
  65
swimming 157–158
swing and rotate drill
  116–117

T

takeoff
  high jump *81,*
    81–82
  long jump 91, *91*
  pole vault *113,*
    113–114, 115
  triple jump
    100–101
takeoff board 89, 91
techniques
  discus *131–133,*
    131–134
  high jump 78–82,
    79–82
  hurdles *30,* 30–33,
    31
  javelin 137–140,
    138–140
  long jump 90–93,
    91, 92
  middle-/long-
    distance races
    47–48
  pole vault
    110–115,
    111–114
  relays 59–62,
    60–62
  shot put 122–125,
    123, 124
  sprints 7–13,
    8–11
  triple jump *100,*
    100–103, *102,*
    103
Teele, Myleik 65
terrain 152, 153
Theodosius 1
third runner
  4 x 100 meter
    relay race 63
  4 x 400 meter
    relay race 64
Thomas, Tracee 93

throw
   discus 132, *133,*
      134
   javelin 139–140,
      140
throwing circle (discus) 131
throwing drills
   arm swing drill
      135
   basketball throw
      drill 142, *142*
   basketball throws
      against a wall
      drill 127
   basketball throws
      for distance drill
      128
   complete throw
      with rubber ring
      drill 135
   discus 135–136
   five-step throw
      with javelin drill
      144
   four-step throw
      drill 142, *143*
   gliding practice
      drill 129
   javelin 142–144,
      142–144
   shot put *127,*
      127–129, *128*
   shot put from
      standing position drill 128
   simple lift drill
      127, *127*
   sitting throw drill
      135
   spin practice drill
      135
   standing throw
      with a javelin
      drill 143, *143,*
      144

step and sling drill
   135
step and throw
   drill 142
wrist flips drill
   127, *128*
throwing events
   120–121. *See also*
   discus; javelin; shot
   put
time travel drill 51
torso bend stretch
   167, *168*
torso twist stretch
   168, 169
tracks 6
trailing leg drill 37,
   38
training
   cross-country
      151–152
   games for 18–19
   goal of xvii
   sprints 6
   weight 151,
      170–173
triathlon 146, **157–159**
triceps pull-downs
   weight training
   exercise 173
triple jump 76,
   99–109
   basics of 99
   drills for *105,*
      105–106, *106*
   faults and fixes for
      104
   introduction as
      women's Olympic event 99
   records in 104
   sample workouts
      for 107–109
   techniques for
      100, 100–103,
      102, 103

troubleshooting. *See*
   faults and fixes
turns
   200-meter race
      11–12
   400-meter race
      11–12
   in sprints 11–12

U

underwater running
   drill 52
uphill runs drill 38,
   51
upright rowing
   weight training
   exercise 172–173
upsweep (baton
   exchange method)
   59–61, *60*
USA Track & Field
   174
U.S. Championships
   44
U.S. Junior National
   Championships
   Michelle Carter in
      126
   Diana Pickler in
      149
   Julie Pickler in
      149
U.S. national records
   4 x 100 meter
      relay races 65
   4 x 400 meter
      relay races 65
   4 x 800 meter
      relay races 65
   100-meter hurdles
      33
   100-meter race 13
   200-meter race 13
   400-meter hurdles
      33

400-meter race 14
800-meter race
  49
1,500-meter race
  49
3,000-meter race
  49
discus 134
high jump 83
javelin 141
long jump 93
pole vault 115
shot put 125
triple jump 104
U.S. Outdoor 119

V

visualization
  160–161

W

Walker, Rachel 141
wall exercise drill
  35, *36*
Walters, Deresa 49
Wang Junxia 49
Washington, B. 65
water 154, 164

weather conditions
  48
websites 174
weight training 151,
  170–173
  guidelines for
    170–171
  for lower body
    171–172
  for upper body
    172–173
Williams, Alycia 65
Williams, Angela 13
Williams, Camee 83
wind resistance 46
Withers, M. 65
Women's Olympics
  2
Women's Sports
  Foundation 174
wood poles 110
World Champi-
  onships
  Stacy Dragila in
    119
  Inger Miller in 69
World Junior Track
  and Field Champi-
  onships
  Diana Pickler in
    149–150

Julie Pickler in
  149–150
world records 33
  4 x 100 meter
    relay races 65
  4 x 400 meter
    relay races 65
  4 x 800 meter
    relay races 65
  100-meter hurdles
    33
  100-meter race 13
  200-meter race 13
  400-meter hurdles
    33
  400-meter race 14
  800-meter race
    48
  1,500-meter race
    49
  3,000-meter race
    49
  discus 134
  high jump 83
  javelin 141
  long jump 93
  pole vault 115
  shot put 125
  triple jump 104
wrist flips drill 127,
  128